"GOD"? What's That?

"GOD"? What's That?

A Translation Guide on "God" for Our God*less* World

༜

PAUL SEUNGOH CHUNG

CASCADE Books · Eugene, Oregon

"GOD"? WHAT'S THAT?
A Translation Guide on "God" for Our God*less* World

Copyright © 2025 Paul Seungoh Chung. All rights reserved. Except for brief quotations in critical publications or reviews, no part of this book may be reproduced in any manner without prior written permission from the publisher. Write: Permissions, Wipf and Stock Publishers, 199 W. 8th Ave., Suite 3, Eugene, OR 97401.

Cascade Books
An Imprint of Wipf and Stock Publishers
199 W. 8th Ave., Suite 3
Eugene, OR 97401

www.wipfandstock.com

PAPERBACK ISBN: 979-8-3852-4410-2
HARDCOVER ISBN: 979-8-3852-4411-9
EBOOK ISBN: 979-8-3852-4412-6

Cataloguing-in-Publication data:

Names: Chung, Paul Seungoh [author].

Title: "GOD"? What's that? : a translation guide on "God" for our God*less* world / by Paul Seungoh Chung.

Description: Eugene, OR: Cascade Books, 2025 | Includes bibliographical references.

Identifiers: ISBN 979-8-3852-4410-2 (paperback) | ISBN 979-8-3852-4411-9 (hardcover) | ISBN 979-8-3852-4412-6 (ebook)

Subjects: LCSH: Apologetics. | God. | Experience (Religion). | Faith and reason—Christianity. | Secularization.

Classification: BT1102 C48 2025 (print) | BT1102 (ebook)

Scripture quotations marked (NIV) are taken from the Holy Bible, New International Version®, NIV®. Copyright © 1973, 1978, 1984, 2011 by Biblica, Inc.™ Used by permission of Zondervan. All rights reserved worldwide. www.zondervan.com The "NIV" and "New International Version" are trademarks registered in the United States Patent and Trademark Office by Biblica, Inc.™

Scripture quotations marked (NRSVue) are taken from the New Revised Standard Version Updated Edition®, copyright © 2021 National Council of the Churches of Christ in the United States of America. Used by permission. All rights reserved worldwide.

Contents

Preface: Calling for Translators, Not Gladiators vii

Prologue: A world where believing in God feels like believing in UFOs 1

PART ONE: What do you mean by "God"?

1. What do you mean by "God"? 15
2. Why "God" is not "god" 25
3. God and Science, the Universe and the Flying Spaghetti Monster 36
4. Everything we say of *everything* comes with a caveat 47

PART TWO: What do you mean God "speaks"?

5. What do you mean God "speaks"? 59
6. What do you mean God "speaks *to* you"? 70
7. What do you mean the Bible is "God's Word"? 82
8. There's truth, then there's truth that generates truths 94

PART THREE: What do you mean God is "good"?

9. Why would you think that God is "good"? 109
10. Why the idea of sin and judgment still haunts us 121
11. Evil is parasitical to God speaking 133
12. Why God still speaks 145

Epilogue: At the crossing of our worldviews 157

Bibliography 161

Preface

Calling for Translators, Not Gladiators

WE LIVE IN A Godless world.

I don't mean that in some moral sense; I mean a world that seems to revolve without "God." We may still believe in God, but that belief is merely *optional*. And the "we" who live here includes everyone, from those who say there's no God and celebrate it to those who are trying to somehow bring God *back* into this world. And the clash of these opposite sides of the spectrum can range from entertaining to disturbing. Most of us though are sort of somewhere in the middle. Some of us may not believe in God, but want to, whereas others of us may believe, but grudgingly. Then, there are those of us who believe there's "*something*," but haven't figured out just *what* that'd be.

However, an even more prominent feature of our Godless world is that we tend to *not actually know* what "God" really means. Of course, we know the dictionary definition: "the supreme being," "the creator of the universe," "perfect in power, wisdom, and goodness." But these are just formulas, equations on a blackboard from a class we never took. We don't know what the word "God" really *points to*.

What most of us have instead are vague impressions, from half-remembered sermons, snippets of something we read, or images from paintings and stained-glass windows. From those, we've imagined a god like "Zeus," or "Odin," from other mythologies, except stronger, wiser, kinder—a Superman version of those gods. But, that god seems *absent* here, in this Godless world, so that even those of us who do believe, often have to remind ourselves that he's *supposed to be* here. Some of us have read the Bible

Preface

of course, but what that two-thousand-year-old book describes is not the world most of us now live in.

And so, we make do in *this* world by trying to connect what we've imagined to be "God" with things and people *here*. But, what are those? Is it the feeling we had on that trip, by that lake, atop that mountain, or in that dimly lit room with a pill of psychedelics? But what about the feeling we had on that dreary day, as we trudged alone, holding a box of personal effects? Is it that kindly nun, tenderly holding a child in her arms? But what about that radio preacher, loudly declaring that our friends are cursed by God? Is it the Big Bang, or the intricate design in Nature? But what about how science makes no mention of "God" for *any* of that? We don't know what points to "God" here; maybe nothing does; or maybe something did and we missed it.

Meanwhile, we still continue to invoke this "God": in the chanting of slogans and slurs in our polarized politics; in yet another eye-rolling cliché about religion in our pop culture; in that YouTube video that says, "Scientist destroys Christianity!" followed by one that says, "Professor pulverizes atheists!" Destroys what, and pulverizes how, I wonder? And what are any of us really chanting about? Our invocations and quarrels often seem to just *flutter* in the wind.

This is not at all to say that there are no meaningful and profound conversations out there about these questions—about God, reality, morality, and such. But too often, we're distracted instead by those of us who perceive such conversations as some kind of gladiator match, with two sides cheering for their champions. Of course, such a match *can* win over *new fans*. But, the fans mostly just root for their own side. Glory to the winner, and death—or, in a kinder world, shame—to the loser! A *performative sport*, except that the scoring schemes seem to be different for each side, so that both sides can say the other side lost.

So, perhaps we need one more thing—one more step—to "prepare the way" for something more. If we who live in a Godless world don't really know what *points to* "God," perhaps our problem is not with the world, but with the language with which we perceive that world.

What if we need *translators*?

We who live in a Godless world need someone to *translate* the world of God. Someone who isn't coming at us like some champion in an arena to defeat our views; someone who isn't selling us their religion; someone who

Preface

knows the lay of our land, and how we speak, to translate for us *what* "God" *means*. Maybe then we could even meaningfully ask *who* "God" is.

This book is my first effort at such translation.

This is not a philosophy or a theology book. Well, it *is* in the topics it explores, but not in the academic sense. And I feel compelled to confess that here, like a penitent before an imaginary clergy of academic rigor: Forgive me, Mother, for I have sinned! I haven't delved into the latest debates in these fields; I've tried to refrain from citing many references; I've played fast and loose with terms; I've used words like how we would in a long conversation under a clear, starry night, with our bellies full from a good meal. And if I couldn't resist elaborating on some scholarly detail, I've usually exiled them into the footnotes.

I want to thank those who enabled me to write this book: My mother and my father, who have urged me to aspire for truth, justice, and love, rather than success—though whether I have, remains to be seen; my brother and my brother-in-faith who have been my steady support; my mentors who directed my studies years ago—one of them is who I imagined when I made my confession; and also those who have listened, read, and engaged me in conversations, writings, and podcasts, which have led to this book. I owe my thanks to many such people. My failures are my own; my virtues are theirs.

And to You who speaks when I ask, "'God'? What's that?"

Paul Seungoh Chung
May 10, 2025

Prologue

A world where believing in God feels like believing in UFOs

THERE IS, IN EACH of us, a voice that speaks our most truthful thoughts. And sometimes it asks us things we don't want to think about.

It spoke up while I was watching the official Pentagon recordings of military encounters with UFOs. It asked: Does this make you believe that there are aliens visiting our planet?

No, I answered. I'd need something much more than this.

But it pressed further: Then, what is that "something"?

I found myself oddly annoyed and replied: Why does that matter? This is not a pressing matter in my life right now.

Still the voice persisted: Well then, what's the difference between you *not* believing in alien UFOs and others *not* believing in God?

I was about to dismiss that question as silly; for God, there's a long history of profound experiences, rational arguments, moral and social.... Then something else spoke, and it spoke with more than words—a sense, a *necessity*: "You need to *properly* answer this question."

There is in each of us a voice that speaks our most truthful thoughts. I won't say this is God speaking. Not *yet*. But, it does point beyond itself *toward* that direction.

WHAT DO WE MEAN BY "WE DON'T BELIEVE"?

I was an agnostic during my early university years. I too, for a time, did not have a belief in God. However, unbelief is a *complicated* thing.

Take our unbelief of UFOs.

Now, I suspect that most of us don't believe that aliens exist—and by that I mean, a full-fledged "there are alien spaceships visiting the Earth" kind of belief. Because if we did, we wouldn't live the way we do. For one thing, we'd consider establishing contact with aliens or setting up UFO countermeasures as key issues for our national elections.

But, what does it really mean for us to *not* believe that aliens exist?

Our nonbelief in aliens, after all, is not so thoroughgoing; there's whole a range of beliefs we hold regarding the possibility of extraterrestrial life. We don't, for example, go so far as to say that there can be no life at all outside our planet; we tend to think that there has to be *some* sort of life out there. And most of us would say that there probably is even some intelligent life *somewhere* among the billions and trillions of worlds in our universe. But, *is* there? Not "there has to be" or "there probably is," but *is* there? And not "somewhere," but *here*—with their UFOs? *That's* what we don't believe; we don't vote based on *that* belief. So far.

So, why don't we? Because it's strange? Weird? Are we imagining little grey men with giant heads? But we know things aren't that simple; why else would some monochrome flight recordings from the government interest us? There's something more to our unbelief concerning UFOs.

It is, for example, different from our unbelief about *Martians*. In the late-nineteenth century, astronomers found what seemed to be canals on Mars, which led some people to believe that there's an alien civilization on that planet. Then, we actually *went there*—or our robots did—and found that there is no such civilization; the canals were optical illusions; the planet was barren. Sci-fi writers may still regale us with imagined tales of things buried deep beneath its red sands, but at least there's no civilization currently on its surface. We found that there are no Martians.

However, we have not likewise found that there are no alien UFOs. If anything, UFOs themselves are real; there really *are* things we've sighted and recorded that so far defy any explanation, which we now categorize as "unidentified anomalous aerial phenomena." But we have yet to find that these things are alien spaceships. Most sightings in the past have turned out to be something mundane, like human aircraft, optical illusions, or a combination of different natural phenomena. So, we assume that even the things we can't explain currently will turn out to be one of those as well. We *assume*; we haven't proved that yet.

So, it's not that we've *positively* found that there's no such thing as alien UFOs. We just don't believe in UFOs. And we feel no need to prove that there are no UFOs, because in a sense, we *have no belief* about them. Our unbelief is simply a "lack" of belief.[1] But, how can we say that we lack a belief regarding UFOs while watching the Pentagon videos?

We can think about it this way. All of us have a set of beliefs we hold and live by—what we call a "worldview." Some of these are consciously held, but many are simply implicit in how we live. We "lack" a belief in alien UFOs when none of these beliefs are about them. We know what UFOs are; we know some people even believe in them. But, our *world*—the world we experience and engage with—decidedly *lacks* alien visitors in spaceships. They don't feature in our considerations; they're not a part of our lives. If pressed, we may say that there's no such thing, but we need not go that far. Our world is simply UFO-*less*; it has no alien UFOs. Instead, it has weather balloons and aircraft, meteors and satellites, optical illusions and sensor malfunctions. And we'll simply assume that an unidentified phenomenon in the sky is one of those things, even when we haven't proved that it is.

This isn't to say that the idea of alien UFOs doesn't interest us. They appear in our stories, movies, and video games. We may even say that we're "*open*" to the possibility that they exist. But we can only be "open" to things that are *not yet inside*. These things are aliens, not just to our planet, but to our worldview—the world we perceive, the world we're living from day to day. And that world continues spinning without them.

That is what it actually means for us to "not believe" in alien UFOs. We think, perceive, and live in a *world* that is UFO-*less*—a world that spins without them. And that is why I needed to answer the question about my unbelief of UFOs, even though I wanted to dismiss it at first.

Because in our secular age—in our secular world—this is how we regard God. The world many of us experience and engage with *lacks* "God"; it is a "God*less*" world.

WHAT DOES IT MEAN TO "NOT BELIEVE" IN GOD, IN A GODLESS WORLD?

Do we really live in a "Godless" world though? After all, one obvious difference between believing in UFOs and believing in God is that a *lot* more people believe in God than they do in alien spaceships. And their belief

---

1. This is what's called "the burden of proof" in philosophy. But, I'm not using this term because I'm not wading into the debate on whether a "lack of belief" in something really exempts you from this burden—from the epistemic responsibility of defending your views. I'm just describing how we seem to think about the question of UFOs.

does impact our society and its laws, or our elections and votes, which can be frustrating, or even disturbing, for those of us who don't believe.

But, in developed nations around the globe, increasingly large portions of the population, especially the younger generations, either do not believe in God or are nonreligious. Among such nations, the U.S. has by far the largest number of those who still believe—mostly Christians—yet even there, that number has fallen drastically in recent years.[2] So, more and more people are living in a world that spins without God. And the main reason they gave for their current views was that they simply no longer believed what their religions taught them.

Now, many of us would say that we left our religious faith for a different reason. We've found deep moral flaws in religious institutions and people; we point to their prejudices, their scandals, their toxic effect on politics and society. But, here's a question: We've also found deep moral flaws in our democracy and its people. Yet, most of us want to *fix* our democracy, not abandon it. So, why this difference?

Again, I'd say that our Godless world lies at the heart of it. Democracy and its ideals are still part of the world we live. Even if its people are flawed, it's still *here, in* our world, to be fixed. Let's say that the plumbing in our house is broken; we'll be angry, but we'll try to fix it. But would we fix it if we believed our house will never have running water? Likewise, if God seems nowhere to be found in the world we experience and engage with—if our world seems to be God*less*—then the failings of the people who believe is not what stops us from believing; it's what stops us *from trying*.

Nor does living in a Godless world mean that we all believe there is no God. We may be militant atheists, rejecting any belief in God; but, we may also be "spiritual but not religious," professing an openness to belief; we may even be troubled Christians, questioning the beliefs we were taught. We may find religious belief to be as weird as believing in little grey men; or we may believe that there is *something* to it. But, that "something" is outside our world, away from our lives, a distant possibility we need not engage with. Living in a Godless world means that we can simply live our lives without any life-shaping belief in God, just as we can do so without having to believe in UFOs.

---

2. For details, see Pew Forum, "Global Religious Landscape," and "Religious Landscape Study," which were conducted in 2012 and 2014, respectively. The most recent study in 2024 found that this trend seems to have slowed in the U.S., but it still concludes that the steep decline of religious belief among its younger generation will leave long-term impact. See Smith et al., "Decline of Christianity."

Prologue

And in that world, we'll come to feel that our unbelief is a simple "lack" of belief. Antony Flew, one of the most influential contemporary philosophers of religion, coined the term "negative atheism" as a contrast to what he called "positive atheism."[3] Whereas a "positive atheist" is someone who positively asserts that God does not exist, a "negative atheist" is someone who is simply *not* a theist. So, "atheists" would include anyone who "lacks" a belief in God, not just those who believe *that* there is no God. And Flew coined this term to argue that it is belief in God that requires proof, *not* unbelief.[4] After all, most of us feel we need an undeniable proof that alien UFOs exist in order to believe; but we don't feel we need an undeniable proof that they don't exist. So, we can live our lives without belief, either in UFOs *or* God, until someone presents us with some "sufficient" proof.

Yet, we can't quite agree on what actually is a "sufficient proof" for God. And this is because our "lack" of belief is not actually a lack; it is a *worldview*. And its Godless world is something *positive*, with parts, weight, and mass.

Take our example of UFOs. Let's say you saw a strange sight in the sky last night. You then learn that an airplane will appear that way when it's night. But you also learn that there's no record of any airplane that flew that night in that part of the sky. Would you conclude that "Though an airplane could have appeared that way, it probably was an alien UFO"? Or, would you think that "Though there's no record of it, it probably was a plane"? Our UFO-less world has *momentum*; a handful of unexplained sightings aren't "sufficient" to stop it from spinning. For us to believe that alien UFOs exist, that world as a whole must come to a screeching halt; it must become unable to spin until we recognize that UFOs are now *inside* that world. And that may take something drastic like alien spaceships landing in our backyards.

So, what would halt our Godless world in its tracks? Perhaps, some life-changing event? A miracle by every measure? That may do it; I personally know a number of people who came to believe in God that way.

But, in asking this, there's something that we who live in this secular age are again failing to remember. Unbelief is a complicated thing. And our unbelief of God is far more complicated than our unbelief of UFOs.

After all, God is *not* a UFO.

---

3. Flew, "Presumption of Atheism," 14, in the footnote.
4. Flew, "Presumption of Atheism," 20.

"GOD"? WHAT'S THAT?

WHAT IF THE "GOD" THAT OUR GODLESS WORLD LACKS IS NOT ACTUALLY GOD?

Here's a question that both those who "lack" a belief in God *and* those who defend that belief often get wrong today. What is the difference between a Godless world and a world with God? Again, consider the example of UFOs. What's the difference between a UFO-less world and a world with UFOs? We may say that the answer is obvious: one has UFOs, and the other doesn't. But that's not quite the complete answer, because each world also has *other things* in it: planets, parallax, pelicans, planes, and so on. Why are these things relevant here? Because when we see a UFO in a UFO-less world, we're mistaking those things for alien spaceships. So, what we should say is that both worlds have the *same list of things*, except that one world *adds* one more thing to the list: alien UFOs.

However, we can't say the same thing in regard to God.

An odd thing happens when we compare a Godless world and a world with God. Both the UFO-less world *and* the world with UFOs agree that something is either an alien UFO *or* something else. If it's one, it's *not* the other: so, it's a parallax effect and *not* a UFO; a pelican and *not* a UFO. And this is the same for a God*less* world. Some thing or event is either God's doing *or* something else: it's evolution and *not* God's creation; a psychological episode and *not* a vision from God. However, in the world with God, things can be *both*: it can be evolution *and* God's creation; a psychological episode *and* a vision from God.

So, if we think that both worlds simply have the same list of things, except that one world just adds God, *we'd be wrong*. Because everything in the list seems to mean something different for each world, at least in regard to God; it's either that or "God" means something different.

We've come to think today that believing in God is about simply "*adding*" God into a world that otherwise have the same list of things, because we think that secular worldviews—our Godless world—emerged by simply "*subtracting*" God from it. The popular story is that science and social progress led us to subtract religious things from our list of beliefs, and that's how our societies became secular. But, that's *not* how it happened. Our most recent historical studies of this time period have largely refuted this "subtraction" story.[5]

---

5. One of the most influential works regarding this topic is by the award-winning philosopher Charles Taylor, who levels a sustained refutation of this "subtraction" story of secularism in his book *A Secular Age*.

Science, progress, or whatever else did not lead us to subtract religious beliefs from our list; rather, we first *changed* what these beliefs *meant*, and how things like science apply to them. And we did so, step by step, over several centuries, by *constructing* new ideas, metaphors, and imageries to re-define the things around us: the world, Nature, and the human self. What emerged then was an entirely different worldview. And this worldview did not simply "lack" a belief in God; it had changed all the relevant terms, including what we even mean by "God."

So, in a book that an atheist journalist reviewed as "the one theology book all atheists really should read," David Bentley Hart observed that most people who debate about God today don't know what "God" actually means. What they tend to mean by "God" is in fact the Demiurge, a cosmic artisan in ancient Greek thought, who made the universe "at some point" by imposing order on the cosmos. But, this Demiurge is *not* God; it is a very powerful being, but *not* "the infinite ocean of being that gives existence to all reality" that Christianity has historically defined as God.[6] During the formative years of secularism in the seventeenth and the eighteenth century, our idea of God became confused with something else: this Demiurge who resides somewhere *outside* the world we experience; a being whose existence we can only *indirectly infer*, from how Nature seems designed, or from why we have morality, and so on.[7] Since then, the "God" that we've been arguing over—the "God" that our Godless world lacks—has *never really been God*.

So, before we can ask what it'd take to believe in God in a Godless world, it seems we'll need to relearn what "God" actually *means*. Except that this raises a new problem for us.

CAN WE REALLY UNDERSTAND WHAT "GOD" MEANS IN A GODLESS WORLD?

Can someone who lives in a Godless world really understand what "God" means? After all, our Godless world can spin without God; but in religions

---

6. Hart, *Experience of God*, 35–36; See also Burkeman, "One Theology Book All Atheists Really Should Read."

7. This view of God is from a philosophical position called deism, which even Christians largely adopted during this time. Taylor too identifies this "deism" as a key shift toward secularism in *Secular Age*, 293–94. Others have made similar assessment, such as Buckley, *Denying and Disclosing God*, 34–69.

like Christianity, without God, *there is no world to spin*. And we don't know what to quite make of that. If what we mean by "God" is something that our world can spin without, then that's *not* really God; yet our Godless world *does* spin without "God" of any sort. What then does "God" mean?

At this point, many of us will ask: What's the problem? Just look up the definition of God, from the Bible, or whatever, and see if our world can spin without adding *that*. But those who confused the idea of the Demiurge with the idea of God did that too. Where did they go wrong? The problem is that we need to learn more than just what the word "God" means by itself; we'd need to learn all the terms, ideas, and beliefs related to it—the *whole worldview*. Because it's understanding those *everything else* that explains *why* our world cannot spin without "God." And it's those *everything else* that we've changed, to construct our Godless world of this secular age. But then, our question becomes no longer about adding God back into our list of things that exist in the world; it becomes about *changing the whole list*.

Our secular, Godless world is now an entirely different worldview from the one that was held by those who believed in God. And different worldviews don't just have different beliefs; they perceive different things; they understand even the same things in a different way. So, in one worldview, a religious vision is a psychological episode; the other, a psychological experience *of* God. For one worldview, Big Bang cosmology makes any belief in a creator unnecessary; for the other, it echoes the Bible's account of creation.[8] So, when people who hold different worldviews debate about what's supposed to be the *same thing*—such as "God"—they tend to talk *past* each other. Because even the same words can mean something different, or refer to different things, or be thought about in a different way.[9] So, a belief held by one worldview often makes no sense to the other. And when it finally *does* make sense, it often no longer means the same thing.

So it is with "God" in our Godless world.

---

8. For example, Stephen Hawking argued for atheism by appealing to Big Bang cosmology, while Georges Lemaître, who first proposed this cosmology, remained a devout Catholic priest, insisting that his theory held no real implication for his faith. For Hawking's view, see Hawking and Mlodinow, *Grand Design*, 180.

9. For a detailed account of this character of worldviews, I recommend Naugle, *Worldview*. For an account that examines how this specifically affects the way we debate about God, I recommend my own book, Chung, *God at the Crossroads of Worldviews*, especially chapters 1–3.

PROLOGUE

And we may be fine with that. It's not like our world will cease to spin because we don't understand some worldview that's very different from our own—a world we just don't live.

Except that our Godless world still has people who hold such views: Christians, Jews, Muslims, and other people who believe in God. And often, we *have* to deal with those people. They may be our neighbors or co-workers. They may even be dear to us: our grandparents, our mom and dad, our spouse, our friends, or even our children. We may find ourselves sitting in their church pews on holidays and special occasions. Or we may just be interested in the beliefs that drive other people. But there's a chasm we can't fully cross. And we sometimes wonder whether even *they* really understand what they believe.

Or perhaps we're on the *other side*. We follow a faith that is profoundly important to us, but we can't make sense of our own beliefs—and not just some hot-button social issues but *core* things, like "God," "creation," "faith," "salvation," and the like. Or, perhaps we are fine with our beliefs, but people around us, people important to us, can't make sense of what we believe. And we want to be *understood*.

Whichever it is, where do we go from here?

WHAT IF WHAT WE NEED IS A "TRANSLATOR" FOR BOTH SIDES?

When I was a child, my family immigrated to Canada from South Korea. So, my first language was Korean; I learned to speak English as a second language. It took about a year for me to freely converse with other kids. But it took several more years for me to become truly fluent. Because I found that language is more than just grammar and vocabulary. Its words and phrases are closely knit with the culture in which they are spoken. The differences in their nuances, the images they conjure, their implicit interconnections—all of these are woven into the language by that culture. So, in a way, our language forms a kind of *world* in which we live. To be fluent in a language is to live in that world, to engage everything *through* it.

I'm now more proficient in English than Korean—I grew up in Canada, after all; but I remain fluent in Korean. And an interesting thing happens when you are fluent in two, vastly different languages, from two very different cultures. It's like there are two different worlds that are *superimposed* over each other. So, for me, when something is being translated from, say

Korean to English, it isn't just about which English words are being used to stand for the original Korean; it's about how the translation and the original are *placed in their respective worlds*.

And we know that translations are about this "placement" because we can sense when a translation of a novel, movie, or anime is bad even when we don't know the original language. Because it doesn't feel natural in *our* language—like it *belongs*. I found that a great translation doesn't just convey the semantic meaning; *it's placed in its world in the same way*; it seems "at home" in its adoptive world, as it is in its original.

But sometimes there are things in one language that are absent in the other. This is usually due to differences in culture: their respective history, ways of life, and so on. Then, how do we translate those? Or *can* we? Here's how: I remarked that when we're fluent in both languages, it's like we perceive two worlds superimposed over each other. So, if there's a word or phrase that seems absent in one language, there's still some portion of the other world that is superimposed over the "same place." There's probably no one-to-one correlation; there may be a number of words or phrases that are only partially there. Yet, there may still be something among them that "overlaps the *most*." What the translator can do is to start with that and then fill in what's still missing with other, partially superimposed portions.

I've been an agnostic and now am again a Christian; I have studied a number of different worldviews—religious and nonreligious. And I found that articulating an idea of one worldview to someone who holds a different one is remarkably like translating. But such a "translation" is not just about conveying the idea's semantic meaning—its definition—but also the sense of its *truth*, its *believability*; it needs to convey why it's believable in its original worldview. And too often, we fail because we simply aren't aware *that* we are translating, so we don't account for how something would "sound" in the other worldview.

But, as with languages, there too is a kind of "fluency" we can reach with a worldview.[10] We learn to perceive and engage everything with it; we

---

10. This is how Alasdair MacIntyre, one of the most significant figures in contemporary English-speaking philosophy, begins to answer the question of how two incommensurable intellectual traditions—what we've called "worldviews"—can meaningfully engage each other. We need someone who is fluent in both traditions, who can explain *why* each side holds the views it does, *in its own terms*. See MacIntyre, *Whose Justice? Which Rationality?*, 160–69. For the application of his answer to how the opposing theistic and atheistic worldviews can meaningfully engage each other regarding the question about God, see Chung, *God at the Crossroads of Worldviews*, chapters 4–6.

learn to *live* in its world. So then, what happens when someone becomes "fluent" in two very different worldviews?

This is much rarer than we'd think. People can know *about* other worldviews, but they rarely live in them. Of course, there are people who have actually changed their worldviews, but most of them were never really at home in their prior world. For example, a Christian who becomes an atheist nowadays tends to be someone who actually lived in a God*less* world, while trying and failing to "add" God into it; the "God" they stopped believing in usually turns out not to be God, but what Hart identified as the Demiurge. This is not to say that there are no people who've had genuine conversions, but I find that those often involved such a life-changing, world-upending experience that they lose their "fluency" with their previous worldview.

People who remain truly fluent in two worldviews have a kind of "dual" vision; the two worlds are *superimposed* over each other, even if they've chosen one world over the other. And they would be able to "translate" ideas and beliefs between the two. We've already read one such translation: unbelief regarding God in a Godless world is rather like an unbelief regarding alien UFOs.

So, here's a question: How would someone who's "fluent" in both a Godless world *and* the world of Christianity translate the belief in God?[11] How would that translation *superimpose* one world to the other? What would we find then? How will our world *change*?

That's the journey on which I want to invite you in this book—embarking from a Godless world to the world of God. Not the entire journey, not even an incursion; just the first steps to its borders where we can *begin* to see the other side, hear its distant sounds, and breathe in its faint air.

Whether you want to explore further will be something we'll decide when we get there.

---

11. Keep in mind that Christianity, as with other major religious traditions, is incredibly diverse in its views. So these "translations" will rarely encapsulate *all* of Christianity's positions regarding that belief. In this book, I'll generally be referring to traditional positions, as articulated by figures like Augustine (354–430), Thomas Aquinas (1225–74), John Calvin (1509–64), and others, who had a wide-ranging and lasting influence on Christian theology. From contemporary works, I will mainly reference Alister McGrath's *Christian Theology*, as it is widely considered to be a representative overview of Christian theology as a whole today.

PART ONE

What do you mean by "God"?

CHAPTER ONE

What do you mean by "God"?

Here's what it's like to live here, in this God*less* world: We've been told that there's this entity called "God," who made this world and watches over us. And we imagined this "God" to be sort of like the gods of other mythologies, like "Zeus" or "Odin," except that just as Superman is to a normal man, so this "God" is to those gods—a kind of "Super-Zeus" who is all-powerful, all-knowing, and perfectly good. Yet, though we've searched high and low, this entity just seems nowhere to be found.

People have pointed to many things in this world as the work of this Super-Zeus. Yet in the same way that the UFOs we've encountered have mostly turned out to be something else, these alleged works of Super-Zeus have also mostly turned out to be something else: evolution, the Big Bang, the human spirit. Maybe there is still this "God" beyond all of that. Or maybe there isn't. Sometimes we wish that such an entity existed, so that he would help us in our darkest times. But in the end we just *make do on our own*. So our world continues spinning without a spinner.

There are times when Superman gets to say, "This is a job for Superman!" Yet in our Godless world, there just seems to be no job for our Super-Zeus—one where he shows up, anyway.

But, *is* "God" really Super-Zeus?

Because if not, what do you mean by "God"?

IS THERE A JOB FOR GOD?

Let me phrase our question more directly. Where would you point to, and say, "That's God at work"? When can we say that we're actually dealing with God?

Perhaps it's when God answers prayers? So, say we pray for someone who's really ill, and they get better. Maybe we can say that that was something God did? But what if it was the doctors and nurses with modern medicine who treated their illnesses? Was it still God then? Because what healed them was medicine, medical professionals, and I suppose the laws of Nature that govern how human bodies heal.

Or, say there's this man who was going through a rough time. And he eventually made it because there was this friend who stood by him, or because some story or a song inspired him in his darkest hours. But then, he later tells us that God saved him. What does he mean? Wasn't it that friend who saved him? Or that story, or that song? Or maybe his own heart that never gave up? Now, it might make some small sense if this friend helped him out because God told him to—whatever that'd mean—but, what if he did it because he was just a good friend?

Of course, people who believe in God say that God can use medicine to heal the sick, or people to help you when you're down. They say that God can work through things and people around us. But that sounds as if God is like this CEO who doesn't actually do anything, while the real job is being done by other things and people.

Maybe we can still say, though, that God is the Creator of everything? But many scientists say that science has made God redundant. That is, science made God lose his job as the Creator, to evolution, the Big Bang, or the laws of physics. So, we can now tell the stories of how life, the universe, and everything came to be through these things, without needing an additional entity like our Super-Zeus god who "started" the whole thing.

Now, there are also many scientists who do believe in God, and they'd say that God can work through things like evolution, the Big Bang, or the laws of physics to create this world. But, again, that sounds as if we're just adding a redundant entity at the top of it all—a CEO who has no real job. An imaginary boss who might as well not exist.

Perhaps then the job for God is to teach us moral laws—how to live a good life, do unto others, that sort of thing. Or maybe it is to bring beauty and meaning into our lives. But, again, those of us who live in a Godless world cannot help but ask: Do we really need some Super-Zeus to act morally or find meaning in life? Isn't our morality simply based on our relation or duty to each other, as human beings? Can we not find or even bring forth meaning in our lives, simply by experiencing the fullness of everything around us, or by drawing deep within ourselves? In other words, are not morality and meaning an intrinsic part of our *human reality*? Why do we need some external entity to dictate these things to us? In fact, what gives this Super-Zeus the right to impose on us *his* standard on what's good or meaningful?

In our Godless world, we are able to tell our stories of what happens around us *without adding* this Super-Zeus entity into our lives.[12] We can do without that addition, because that entity plays no real role; there's no "job" for him.

That's why many of us no longer believe in God today. And even those of us who still do, tend to think of God only when something happens and there's no explanation for it. So we say it's God if we're healed and the doctors don't know how; we say it's God when we have some unexplainable religious experiences; we'll say, "God did it," if we think that scientists cannot explain where life ultimately came from, or what "caused" the Big Bang. We speak of God in those unreached corners of reality where we can still say, "This is a job for Super-Zeus!"

Yet, what do we do if we figure out what happened in all of those cases? Would that mean that even an all-powerful entity like God will become unemployed? Is that when our age-long belief that such an entity is out there, somewhere, finally departs from us?

However, we've missed something here. We were so caught up on whether or not we can find a job for this entity that we've been getting this one crucial thing *wrong*.

According to Christianity, God is *not* an entity.

---

12. *The Miracle of Theism* by J. L. Mackie, which has become a contemporary classic for atheistic philosophy, sums up this view with the following words: "We can agree with what Laplace said about God: we have no need of that hypothesis" (253). Mackie regarded belief in God as "any view that adds a god . . . to the world" (251) and argued that our "explanation . . . of reality" has no need to "postulate [that] entity" (250).

GOD IS NOT AN ENTITY—NOT EVEN ONE LIKE "SUPER-ZEUS"

Here's a provocative, yet curiously traditional, formulation for God in Christianity: "God is not *a* being," it goes, "God is Being-itself."[13]

Both Jews and Christians have always believed that God is the Creator of literally *everything*: not just things like rocks and people, but even things like space and time. But this claim was saying more than that God was some uniquely powerful entity who made our world, like the ancient Greek "Demiurge." Because, according to the Bible, this literal "everything" not only came into existence by God's power but also *continues to exist by that same power*.[14] If God were to cease exerting that power, everything would simply *cease to exist*. So they concluded that God is the Creator not simply as "*a* being" that made the world but as the constant "*ground of being*" of everything, from rocks and people to space and time.

But what does that even *mean*? At this point, some of us may find our eyes glazing over at what seems to be an obscure religious technicality. However, this is far more than that.

After all, the reason why we think that God has no role in our world is because we're thinking of God as just another entity, even if one that is all-powerful and all-knowing, like our Super-Zeus. Because of this, God has become for us something that exists *alongside* everyone and everything else, like gravity, lions, or people. God has become just one of the possible characters—albeit a unique one—auditioning for a role in the stories we tell about our reality: stories of how people were saved, or how life came to be, or how the universe began. And he can fail the audition, or, all the roles could've been taken already.

Of course, none of this helps us to understand this strange formulation for God. So, since we've brought up this analogy of "stories," let's go with that.

In a story like *Hamlet*, where is the author? Where's Shakespeare? In one sense, *nowhere*. Shakespeare is nowhere to be found in the world of

---

13. This specific formulation is from Tillich, *Systematic Theology*, 1:237. Many of Paul Tillich's views remain controversial among Christians despite his enormous influence, but his statement, "God is being-itself, not *a* being," is well-established in traditional Christian theology. It's found, for example, in *Summa Theologiae* (Henceforth, *ST*) by Aquinas, who states that God is "not in a genus"—not *a* being—but is "the principle of all being" (*ST* I.q3.a5).

14. See, for example, Job 34:14–15 and Heb 1:3.

What do you mean by "God"?

Hamlet. That's because the author does not typically exist anywhere as an entity *inside* their story. But, in another sense, he is *everywhere*, because the entire story *is* the author—or rather, their words. Then, what is the author's role in the story? What does Shakespeare do in *Hamlet*? Again, in one sense, *nothing*. Everything that happens in a story happens because of the characters, circumstances, and forces that exist *inside* that story. Yet, in another sense, what the author does is *everything*, because everything that happens in the story is the author's words. And authors unfold their stories through everything and every happening inside their stories, rather like how religious people say that God "works through" all things, like medicine, people, evolution, or the Big Bang.

Now, the obvious question from our Godless world will be: "But why should we believe that our world has an author outside of it?"

However, in asking that question, we're *still* likely thinking of God as some Super-Zeus entity. Because although authors do not exist as entities inside their stories, they do exist as entities *outside*, living their own lives. And here's where we've hit the limit of our metaphor. God is like an author. But there is no "*outside*" to *God*'s story.

If we're to find that we are all inside some made-up story—perhaps a computer program like the Matrix—what's happening in the world "outside" would *still be God's story*. And our made-up world would remain as part of God's story too, as a story told within a larger story, like the tales of Scheherazade in *One Thousand and One Nights*. And outside, as well as inside, God would not be an entity, but "being-itself"—the "ground of being"—of each and *every* world.

And most of us today just can't make sense of this idea. We've been living, thinking, and conversing in a Godless world, where "God" is an entity outside. So, if there is no "outside" to that world, we'll ask why we'd need such an entity as the "ground of being," or whatever else.[15] We simply aren't familiar with the kind of worldviews that would've made sense of this. And this includes, ironically, many Christians today.

What we have here then is a problem of translation.

So, let's try this. Pretend that we don't know what the word "God" means; in fact, if by "God" we're still thinking of some "Super-Zeus" entity,

---

15. Even a highly read philosopher like Mackie remarked that this God of traditional Christian theology, represented by "Hume's Demea," "provides no purchase for reasoning" (*Miracle of Theism*, 243). He then goes straight to the framework he's familiar with, by arguing that "to postulate an entity" (250) even such an "indeterminate and mysterious a god," as an explanation of reality is "needless as it is incomprehensible" (251).

we really *don't* know. For now, forget that God is "the Creator," or "all-powerful," "all-knowing," "perfectly good," or even "loving."

Instead of "God," here's a word that *translates* the idea into the language spoken in our Godless world. Think of this, though, as a low-resolution translation—a rough sketch just to start us off.

Because we don't know, we ask: "What do you mean by 'God'?"

And the reply is: *"By 'God,' we mean, 'Reality.'"*

"GOD" IS "REALITY"—A TRANSLATION

To be precise, by "God" we mean "reality" at the most fundamental *and* comprehensive level, with its infinite variations and possibilities, both immediately experienced and beyond all experience.[16] But, let's keep the translation simple here.

God is *Reality*.[17]

No, I do *not* mean that God is the universe. That would be a wrong translation. The word "reality" is both more immediate *and* more encompassing.

Let's think about how we relate to reality.

We are *always* engaged with reality, are we not? We engage reality in everything we do. Reality is what we're exploring in *any* scientific inquiry. And don't we say things like "You need to look at reality"? Because what we believe and do are measured against reality. And most of us don't think that reality is so *permissive* that we can do whatever we want, believe whatever we wish, and get away with it. *That's* why we think something's true and something's false.

Literally everything that happens is what Reality unfolds, which encompasses *all of history*, of the cosmos, life, humanity, or even other universes—if there are such things. So, we all live, do what we do, and be what

---

16. In his incisive critique against how we misunderstand the idea of God today, Hart presents a similar corrective definition of God as the "ultimate reality that the intellect and the will seeks [and] the primordial reality with which all of us are always engaged in every moment of existence and consciousness" (*Experience of God*, 10).

17. Generally speaking, I'll use the capitalized "Reality" to denote this infinite, comprehensive, and fundamental level, while using the uncapitalized "reality" to denote that part of "Reality" *we* are engaging and experiencing. But, for our purposes in this book, both are essentially interchangeable.

we are, *in* Reality. Or as the apostle Paul puts it in the Bible, "For in [God] we live, move, and have our being."[18]

Reality and what it unfolds presents us with both the beauty *and* the tragedies of life, both the good *and* the evils of our world. Yet—and this is especially important—it also presents us with our *moral sense*, including how we came to develop or evolve this sense as a species. And this has made us aspire for what is good and to overcome what is evil, to love beauty and endure tragedies. This is how we've discovered meaning, either within or beyond ourselves. All of that is *part of Reality*.

This in turn means that Reality encompasses not only everything "outside of us" but also everything "inside of us": our inmost thoughts and feelings; how and why our hearts and minds are the way they are; things we yearn for, things we wrestle with, things we aren't even aware of. Just as we're engaged with the reality of what's *around us*, so too we're engaged with the reality of what's *within us*.

We also need to remember that what we mean by "Reality" is more than just the total *sum* of what exists *now*. Because new things can emerge in our world, entirely new kinds of existence that never existed before, like how life or consciousness arose from inanimate matter. "Reality" means more than just "the universe," because its story encompasses how the entire universe *came into existence*—even how there can be "other universes," utterly different from our own. Hence, "Reality" is the *Infinite*—an infinity of what is *and* what can be. That is why we can come up with new ideas, make innovations, or forge paths where there were none before; we discover and draw upon the limitless possibilities that Reality holds. So, in a real sense, as we engage reality, reality *reveals to us* what's possible.

So, whenever we're reaching for some distant dream, or striving toward some moral ideal, or searching for some unknown truth, what we're really doing is engaging reality. And others may discourage us by saying—in fact with the very words—"look at reality." But, when we prove them wrong and succeed, we are vindicated by reality; our engagement was *tested* and *judged by it*, so to speak.

All of this is just how it is, no matter how powerful, wise, or great we are. We could be a superhero, or a hyper-advanced alien whose civilization spans a thousand galaxies. We could even be a god. Yet Reality is what's all around us and within us, what we engage and interact with at all times, and what judges everything we do.

---

18. Acts 17:28a.

"God"? What's That?

And everything—*everything*—we've just said about "Reality" is what people who believe in God have said of "God." This is how they related to God in their everyday life. All of that is what "God" really meant.

This is why a church father of western Christianity confessed that God is "the Truth" that is "more inward to me than my innermost, and higher than the utmost high."[19] And subsequent Christian theologians put this into words in the following formulas: God is "Being-itself, not *a* being"; likewise, God is "Truth-itself" and "Goodness-itself."[20] God is not simply an entity that knows every truth; God *is* Truth. God is not just an entity that is perfectly good; God *is* Goodness. Even today, Christians often quote that Bible verse, "God is Love."[21] Not just that God is loving, but that God *is* Love.

So, our translation: God is not an entity *in* Reality; God *is* Reality.

That's why there's no job for God. God is not out of a job due to some recent downturn in our metaphysical economy; rather, God *is* the Economy. We need not ask when God plays a role in our lives, because God is—Reality is—what every one of us are engaged with at *all times*.

Or in the words of a psalm, sung by ancient Hebrews in the Bible:

> O LORD, Where can I go from your Spirit?
> Or flee from your presence?
> If I go up to the heavens, you are there;
> If I make my bed in the depths, you are there.
> If I settle on the far side of the sea,
> even there you will guide me.
> If I say, "Surely the darkness will hide me,"
> Even the darkness will not be dark to you.[22]

---

19. Augustine, *Confessions* 3.6. In Latin, "interior intimo meo et superior summo meo."

20. This formulation, which also includes "Unity" and "Beauty," is referred to as the Divine transcendentals. This idea was developed and fully articulated by medieval theologians, with the most significant example found in Aquinas's discussion of God's attributes, particularly Being (*ST* I.q3), goodness (*ST* I.q5-6), truth (*ST* I.q16), unity (*ST* I.q3.a7), and beauty (*ST* I.q5.a4); For a contemporary discussion on this topic, see Aertsen, *Medieval Philosophy and the Transcendentals*.

21. 1 John 4:8, 16.

22. Psalm 139:7-12a.

What do you mean by "God"?

"GOD IS REALITY" IS AN INCOMPLETE TRANSLATION

There's a problem with this translation, however. If by "God" we simply mean "Reality," then *everyone* believes in God.[23] But clearly, we don't. What we mean by God can't *only* mean "Reality." Because if so, what would it even mean to disbelieve in God?

Our translation is *incomplete*. However, *it's not a wrong translation*—one that implied that God was "Super-Zeus," an entity *in* our reality, even if a unique one. And it clarifies the real question that we should've been asking, which is: What is the most adequate understanding *of* Reality? What's the best portrait of Reality, so speak?

And this is where we can begin to perceive the real difference between those of us who believe in God and those of us who don't. It's not about believing or disbelieving that there's an all-powerful entity somewhere in our reality; it's about *how to relate to reality as a whole*.

Or, to put it differently, our disagreement is not about whether to add some Super-Zeus god into the "picture" of reality before us; rather, that picture itself is *ambiguous*—like the famous duck-rabbit, or the old lady-young lady images—and we're arguing about what we're seeing. And the ambiguity we're arguing over is this: Is Reality a *Who* or a *What*?

That's the real question. God is a *Who*; we relate to God as a *"Thou,"* not an *"It."*[24] If by "God," we mean "Reality," then the central problem for our belief in God is not that God seems nowhere to be found, but that "God"—reality we're engaged with at all times—does not seem to care, or worse, is *incapable* of caring. So, is Reality *personal*?

It's at this point that some of us will jump to questions like whether there seems to be a purpose or design to our universe. That would be far too hasty, however. After all, it turned out that most of us didn't know what

---

23. This parallels Hart's explanation of Anselm's ontological argument: Disbelieving God in this sense would be like saying that "Being lacks being or that Reality is not real" (*Experience of God*, 122); Mackie has been the main spokesperson in this chapter for our Godless world, so I'll have him speak here again: "That there is *some* reality is beyond doubt. The extreme of nihilism would be to deny that reality is discoverable or understandable; but there is no serious case for this denial" (*Miracle of Theism*, 245). What Mackie is pointing out here is that no one, not even a nihilist, can deny that there *is* reality; what a nihilist denies is that *we can meaningfully engage* reality. Then he rejects even this denial, while insisting that an atheist has no need of God to do so.

24. This specific formulation is from Martin Buber's influential work. See Buber, *I and Thou*, 75–76.

"God" really meant. Why would we then think that we already know what it really means to say that Reality—that God—is personal?

To learn what *that* means, we'd need to first follow the story of how the Jews and then the Christians have engaged what our Godless world have been calling "Reality." And it is a story that spans many, many generations—a tapestry woven by different people, perspectives, and personalities. There were many key events, experiences, and insights, and more importantly missteps, mistakes, and misunderstandings. It is through this long history of engagement that they came to relate to reality as a *Who* that engages them—a Who with a particular *personality*.

However, we won't be following that story in *this* book, other than in bits and pieces. That's because we *can't*; we don't speak its "language"; we need translation. And we have yet to translate even its most basic "vocabulary." For example, the Bible reports that God "spoke to Abraham." But what does that *mean*? What did someone like Abraham experience, and why would they believe that *that's God speaking*? Likewise, there are other relevant key words that we likely don't understand while naively assuming we do, such as what it really means to say that God "created the universe," or that God is "good," or that the Bible is the "Word of God." We will now explore these questions in turn, which will enable us to understand that millennia-long story and journey into its world.

For this is a translation guide on "God" for our Godless world.

CHAPTER TWO

Why "God" is not "god"

Before we can translate more vocabulary about "God" though, we'll need to clear away some remaining debris of our present misconceptions. We've been living in a Godless world, and we still think, unthinkingly, with its confused habits.

Here's one example: Why do we think the word "God" is capitalized? And most of us today tend to think that this is just how monotheistic religions like Christianity refer to their god. If that's so, it'd be rather haughty of them, calling the gods of other religions, like Zeus or Odin, mere "gods," while capitalizing *their* god. Some of us even try to redress this seeming injustice by removing the capital from the Christian "God." We may, after more thought, add that unlike those other gods, "God" is supposed to be the all-powerful and all-knowing Creator of the world. And that brings us back to the Super-Zeus god, a uniquely powerful entity *inside* Reality.

Yet, God is not an entity *in* Reality; God *is* Reality; "God" is the very reality we're engaged with, *everywhere* and at *all times*. At least, that was our starting translation.

But then, where does this leave us? Is "God," well, "god" in any sense of the word? Because if not, why *that* word? Why g-o-d? This is the first debris we'll need to clear: the confusion regarding the relationship between "God" and "god."

"GOD"? WHAT'S THAT?

WHAT IT WAS LIKE TO BELIEVE IN "GODS"

We'll want to start by exploring what it was like to hold a belief in gods in the first place. Except that's an impossible task. Belief in gods is far too complex and diverse to explore in any single book. So, let's focus on just one point, which I will illustrate in the following.

Imagine yourself as a citizen-soldier of one of the Greek city-states about twenty-five hundred years ago. You're in the midst of battle; sharp sounds of weapons clashing, screams of the wounded and the dying, are ringing all around you. Your leaders claimed that your enemies were craven cowards; they were wrong. And now you see your countrymen in the lines in front of you falling back, as one after another is struck down. Panic, like a wave, is washing over you and your fellow soldiers. Some men in your unit are already breaking ranks and fleeing from the field, ignoring the frantic orders from your commanding officer.

Maybe you should run too. But can you live with the shame back at home? Besides, it's likely that you'll be overtaken and slain anyway. As you stand, unable to decide, the enemy hoplites charge toward your line. You grip your spear tightly with your right hand, your shield with your left, as beads of sweat run down your face beneath your helmet. Fear grips you. You don't want to die. You don't want to die. Someone beside you goes down with an arrow in his throat. You think you recognize who he is, but you can hardly think. Everything's a blur. You don't want to die. *You don't want to die.* Spears flash, and blow after blows batter your shield. And you snap. *No!* Your vision goes red. You will kill *them!* You roar and thrust your spear at the screaming man in front of you. At least, you'll take them down with you!

You are in the grip of Ares, the god of war. Ares is moving amidst this battle; his sons, Phobos and Deimos—fear and panic—are running madly before him.

Let me make this clear. You do not merely believe that there's a god named Ares who resides in some divine realm, overseeing this battle; your belief is not simply an *intellectual position* that there's an entity in charge of warfare. You are *experiencing* the god of war in *this* battle. The clash of arms, terror, violence, valor—all of that is *Ares himself.* You *see* this god in the carnage around you; you *hear* him in the battle cries of your friends and foes; you *feel* the scourge of his sons, fear and panic. This battle *is* Ares, the god of war.

Why "God" is not "god"

Of course, you also know that this battle is, well, a battle—with men at arms, supplies, tactics, strategies, and violence. Your comrade, dead on the ground, is not Ares. A spear held in your hand is not Ares. But, at the same time, *all of that* is Ares. You *perceive* this god in the battle, because war and carnage *is* Ares.

People in the ancient past did not merely believe that gods "existed"; they *perceived* them in what happened around them. To go to war is to march with the god of war; to fall in love is to be touched by the goddess of love; to look at the sun is to see the sun-god; to harvest crops is to receive them from the goddess of the earth. And if you're thinking that we now know that these gods do not "really exist," because we have a scientific understanding of our world, you'd be failing to understand how they thought about these things.

Again, let's say you're an ancient Greek soldier, and a plague was sweeping through your army camps. You'd believe that Apollo, the god of the sun, music, prophecy, and disease—a rather complicated combination—is shooting his arrows at your countrymen, for whatever reason. Now, if someone from our time brought you a microscope and *showed* you the microbes that are causing this sickness, it wouldn't change what you believe. I do *not* mean that you'll just refuse to look into the microscope, stubbornly insisting that Apollo's arrows are making people sick. I mean that if you were persuaded to look, and you saw these tiny things called "microbes," you'll think that these things *are* Apollo's arrows. The ancient Greeks knew very well that sick people don't have literal arrows sticking out of them. Whatever is making people sick are invisible, but somehow "like" an arrow, bringing down people from a distance, and now, you would be *seeing* these invisible, arrow-like things.

What may change is your view on *how* or *why* people are "struck down by the arrows of Apollo." Learning about disease vectors, contagion, and so on, will tell you that there's a pattern to things—cause and effect—such as *how* disease spreads. And we didn't need modern science for this kind of thinking. In the ancient world, including Greece, *philosophy*, which eventually gave rise to modern science, developed the view that there is a rational principle for everything, from the movement of the stars to the composition of matter, from individual human morality to the ways society is to be organized and governed.

But none of this made people stop believing in their gods. In ancient Greece, philosophy simply made some of them *see* their gods in a *different way*. In their old stories, their gods were capricious—sometimes cruel, sometimes benevolent, all depending on their whims. But, with philosophy, they began to perceive the divine *in the rational order* of the world. Not all of them, of course; there were as diverse views about the gods as there were different schools of thought. But Platonism, the most prominent position, presented the gods as principles and patterns of the cosmos—personal beings that manifest the different threads woven into the ordered tapestry of our reality. And so, Plato wrote: "All things are full of gods."[1]

EARLY CHRISTIANS WERE CONSIDERED "ATHEISTS" BY THEIR CONTEMPORARIES

It was to this world and its way of thinking that Christians first professed their belief in God. And one reason why the early Christians were persecuted so severely by the Roman Empire was because they were thought to be *atheists*.

Because to the Romans, who regarded themselves as the heirs of Greek civilization, Christians seemed to be rejecting this very world—a world "full of gods." After all, they did not worship the official gods of the empire—the Roman version of the Greek gods; nor did they worship the emperor as a god among them. Instead, they only worshipped *their* god as the "one true God."

It has been nearly two thousand years since then, and the gods of ancient Rome are no longer worshipped in their homeland. The Vatican, the center of Roman Catholic Christianity, stands at the heart of Rome. And nearly a third of the human population align themselves with Christianity, with a quarter more with Islam, which claims to also worship this god. So, it seems that it is Christians and their god who have triumphed in the end.

If so, it is a victory that is now waning. For the world that was once "full of gods" we could perceive has become today a God*less* world in which we can find no god. And even the Christian god seems to be losing his place in this new world. Some of us may consider this to be a kind of poetic

---

1. Plato, *Laws* 10.899b. See also Tarnas, *Passion of the Western Mind*, 13–15. This widely read book by Richard Tarnas presents a broad overview of Western intellectual history, from ancient Greek worldviews and philosophy to our "postmodern" era. His book has been popular for presenting a good digest of this history, though its overview overlooks the kind of secular "mistranslations" of the idea of God we want to correct in this book.

justice, and quip, "Most of us don't believe in gods like Zeus or Odin anymore; I just don't believe in one more god."

However, this characterization of what happened misses one crucial step. It wasn't that Christians were simply rejecting the gods of all other peoples, wanting only their god to remain. It wasn't even that they just believed that there is only one god, rather than many gods. Neither was *quite* what they were up to. Centuries before Jesus Christ lived and taught on the eastern edge of the Roman Empire, in a province named Judea, Jews who had lived there had been re-defining their idea of "God." And Christians, who were born from their faith, continued this journey until the gods of the peoples around them no longer fit what they meant by "God."

And Christian theology can now articulate the difference between the two ideas more clearly.[2] The "gods" are powerful entities that reside in some higher, greater realm. There are many such "gods," as many as there are different parts to our world, from Nature, society, to our own inner life—as many as there are roles to play in the larger story of our reality. Yet the "God" that Christians speak of does not point us to anything *in* our reality, but to *reality as a whole*; not to *a* character inside some cosmic story, but to the *entire story* that is unfolding.

So, in a sense, Christians *were* atheists. For the "God" they worshipped was *not* a "god."

THE JOURNEY FROM THE "GOD OF ISRAEL" TO "GOD"

This is not at all to say that there is no relation between the idea of "God" and the idea of "gods." The Jewish and the Christian idea of God probably began as something that wasn't very different from what peoples around them believed about their own gods. I say "probably" because what we say about how the idea of God developed over time is a reasoned *re-construction* by scholars today; it's like a piece of Ikea furniture we assembled, but it still has missing parts and leftover screws and bolts. And what we'll cover here is a simplistic summary of *that*.[3]

Our account begins with the ancient Israelites, who in time, would write down what we now call the Hebrew Bible—or the Christian Old Testament. Their "god" was the one that their ancestors encountered, and

---

2. For a contemporary example, see Hart, *Experience of God*, 28–34, 94–95.

3. For recent, widely read scholarly books that present a survey of the subject, see Smith, *Early History of God*; Day, *Yahweh*.

who formed a personal relationship with them. They called this god, "*Yahweh*"—in the English Bible, it is written as "the LORD." And they would follow the laws and commands of this god, and he would protect them and guide them. These Israelites do not seem to have believed that their god was the only god per se; several times in the Bible, they seem to believe that other nations had their gods too. However, the Israelites—or at least, some of them—committed themselves to following only Yahweh as their god. They recognized that it was this god who had, time after time, rescued them from foreign enslavement and oppressions, because of the promise he made with their ancestors.

This ancient Israelite belief in Yahweh took form within the framework of surrounding Canaanite religion and culture. What the Canaanites believed regarding their gods was, at times, integrated into the Israelite belief in their god, and at other times rejected. Especially significant was the Canaanite belief in a god named "El," who was said to be creator of the cosmos and the father of their gods and goddesses. In the Bible, "*El*," is a Hebrew word for "god," and seems to be an early name of God; it appears inside the names like Dani*el*, Samu*el*, Micha*el*, and of course, Isra*el*.[4]

Scholars theorize that the ancient Israelites identified Yahweh with El; so, the god who has rescued them was also the god who created the world. Then, over time, the Israelites would attribute powers and domains of other Canaanite gods and goddesses to this god, Yahweh-El.

What they believed about their god was further refined and expanded during the history of their nations, Israel and Judah, and their later Jewish remnants. The civilizations of Egypt and Babylon were sources of many imageries and ideas in the Bible. Zoroastrian teachings likely influenced the Jewish thoughts on God after their nation was absorbed into the Persian Empire. And centuries later, Greek philosophy had profound influences on Christian thought. Of course, all this is not very different from how modern science and philosophy are key dialogue partners for theologians today in how they think about God. Yet, the Israelite belief in their god held an inner logic that unfolded the idea of God from these influences in a particular way.

They believed that their god was the Creator of the world. Yet, what did that mean? Did this god create only certain things, or everything? The

---

4. According to Exod 6:3, God appeared to the ancestors of Israel, Abraham, Isaac, and Jacob, *as "El-Shaddai,"* translated into English as "God almighty." In Gen 14:18–20, Melchizedek, a Canaanite king who blesses Abraham, is called the priest of "El-Elyōn," translated as "God Most High."

ancient peoples around Israel believed that the gods who made the world had to battle the primordial monsters of chaos that dwelt in the depths of the sea. Every night, Ra, the supreme sun-god of Egypt, battled Apep, the serpent of darkness that lurked in the deep; Marduk became the king of the gods of Babylon, for slaying the dragon-mother Tiamat that rose from the sea. Likewise, there are mentions in the Bible about how the god of Israel slew the great sea-serpent Leviathan; however, the Bible also declares that the same god *created* the Leviathan and the great monsters of the deep, granting them their own place in the world.[5] This poses a question: What does it mean for a god to create *everything*, including the monsters that other gods had to engage in a terrifying battle to the death?

Another way the idea of God unfolded was from their belief that Yahweh directed the course of history. Ancient peoples perceived their gods in what immediately happened around them. Specifically, victories and defeats, fortune and ruin, rise and fall of individuals or people, were something that their gods brought about. So, if your nation was defeated, it meant that you'd lost the favor of your gods *or* that your gods were weaker than the gods of your enemies. But this belief would unfold in a different direction for the Israelites.

The prophets of Israel and Judah had frequently warned that their god, Yahweh, was not a mere national deity who would protect them in exchange for their acts of religious devotion. "I desire mercy, not sacrifice," their god declared. "Act justly, love mercy, and walk humbly with your God."[6] If his people were unjust and corrupt, their god would bring judgment upon them, and even appoint their enemies to defeat them. And when the kingdoms of Israel and Judah were destroyed by foreign empires, their warning seemed to have come true. Of course, other peoples also believed that their gods judged them for their actions. Yet, the prophets of Yahweh went a step further. They declared that their god judges not only Israel and Judah, but *every* nation and people *in the same way*—and not just people, but *their gods* as well.[7]

Then, as history unfolded, the empires that destroyed their nation were, in turn, destroyed. And then, Persia, a seemingly more benevolent

---

5. Compare Ps 74:13–14 to Ps 104:25–27. See also Gen 1:21–22, which reports that God created the "*tannin*," along with all other creatures of the sea and the sky. "*Tannin*" is the Hebrew word for great sea monsters, like Leviathan, and God even *blesses* them to flourish.

6. Hos 6:6; Mic 6:8.

7. Exod 12:12; Ps 82; Isa 46:1–2; Jer 46:25; 50:2.

empire, rose to power and restored the ancestral land of Israel to their Jewish descendants. So, these Jewish remnants were confronted with a new question: What does it mean for a god to unfold history, and judge *all* nations, which presumably had their own gods?

Is the Creator of *everything*, the one that unfolds *all of history*, and judges *all peoples*, along with *their gods*—is such a god, really like any other god?

WHERE THAT JOURNEY LED: THE NAMES OF GOD

Names are important. They set you apart from others. Paul is not Peter or Patrick; Phoebe is not Priscilla or Patricia. Names can connect you with roles and domains: Paul the evangelist; Patrick the saint of Ireland. And all this was even more so with the names of gods.

Names set the gods apart from each other: Zeus is not Apollo or Ares; Ra is not Tefnut or Hathor. Names connected them with distinct domains and roles: Zeus is the sky, Ra is the sun, Tefnut the rain and water; Hathor the dancing of stars, Apollo the healing of ills, Ares the waging of war. Their roles told the ancients just "where to look" to perceive their gods; their domains implied how to rank them in a hierarchy—greater domain with greater power, and the greatest as their king. That's how we've placed our gods inside our reality, each according to their names.

But then, we have the Jewish and the Christian name for God—and later, Islam as well. Their "god" is simply called "God." *Allah*, by the way, literally means "The God."

And "God" is a very odd name in that it isn't a name at all. It gives no distinction. It does not come with any domain or role. It's curiously *undefined*. In English, it's "God," and it's the same with every other language. "*Gott*" in German, "*Deus*" in Latin, "*Theos*" in Greek, and even in Japanese, "*Kami-sama*." And all of them simply mean "God."

The Hebrew word for "God" in the Bible is "*Elohim*." It literally means "gods," plural, as in *all the gods*. It comes from "El," the Canaanite creator god, who ruled the other gods; so, the word referred to El and all the gods in his divine council. And in the Bible, "Elohim" can mean just that: the many gods of other nations. But the same word is also used for the god of Israel; it is "Elohim" who creates all things and rules all creation; it is "Elohim" who is "Yahweh." And when "*Elohim*" is used in that sense, the verb that follows is *singular*. So, the word the Bible uses the most to refer to "God" is singular,

Why "God" is not "god"

yet uses a word that refers to all the gods. That's because "God" in the Bible is not a god *of* anything, but the "god" of *everything*. There is no particular domain or role or place in a hierarchy for *this* god. This god is simply "God."

There is, of course, still the name, "Yahweh." And that name did set the god of Israel apart from the other gods. But it turns out that the meaning of that name raises the same issue. According to the Bible, the name "Yahweh" means "I am that I am," or "I will be what I will be," or "I cause to be what I cause to be."[8] Yet this phrase is again strangely *undefined*; it points us to what is unbounded and unlimited, to anything and everything.

These two names were the answers to the questions regarding their god that the Jewish descendants of the Israelites wrestled with: *Who* or even *What* is their god? They perceived this god in how *all* of history unfolded. But that also meant that their god was not bound to this or that people or nation, not to their rise or fall, or to their time or land. They perceived this god in *everything*. But this also meant that their god was not this or that thing, not the sky, or the sun, or the stars, or the storm, or the sea, neither life nor death, neither peace nor war. Rather, *all* of that, and history itself, was what their god was *doing*. So, the names of their god point to everything that is and everything that can be—in a word, to "Reality."

Long ago, their ancestors had encountered a god. And they worshipped him like other peoples did with their gods. But that "god" then broke the very frame within which humanity had placed their gods. Their god was something *more* and *beyond*. The *Infinite*. "God," not a god.

THE CHRISTIAN SEARCH FOR "GOD" THAT IS NOT "A GOD"

Still, this idea of "God" could've been reduced to a mere "super" version of a god—a Super-Zeus. After all, that's what we've done today. But an interesting thing happened when Christians professed their belief in God to a world that was "full of gods."

When the early Christians were accused of atheism, and persecuted by the Roman Empire, a Christian philosopher named Athenagoras wrote a letter to the emperor titled, "Plea for the Christians." He explained that Christians were not atheists; they believed in "God who made the universe." Yet, he did not defend Christianity from the accusation of atheism

---

8. Exod 3:14. See also Stone, "I Am Who I Am," 624. To be precise, "Yahweh" does not *literally* mean "I am that I am," etc. Rather, the name seems to be closely connected with, or even derive from, this Hebrew phrase.

by simply saying that they believed in a god greater than the gods of Greece and Rome; he argued that Greek and Roman philosophers, from Plato to Aristotle to the Stoics, taught about this "God" as the Source of all things, even if they used different names.[9] And he was not the first to take this approach. This is how apostle Paul argued during his speech at Athens, which is recorded in the book of Acts in the Bible. He begins by telling the Greek intellectuals listening to him that he will talk about a new god. But he then points out that their own philosophers already spoke about this "God," as the Creator of all things, "in whom we all live, move, and have our being," so that all of us "are his offspring."[10]

The "God" that Jews and then Christians were professing was *like* a god, speaking and engaging with humanity *personally*. But that was the limit of this comparison. This "God" was not some greater god, but a different level of reality altogether—the most comprehensive and the most fundamental. If gods really existed, they would exist *within* and *by* this Reality. This "God" was the Truth to which these gods would be measured; the Goodness by which they would be judged. This "God" was *one*, not in the sense that there's only one such entity, but in the sense that the Infinite is "one," the Source of all things is "one," and that Reality is "one."

And when Christian professed their belief in God to the peoples around them, they were searching the other religion or culture for something that resembled their own journey from the "gods" to "God." And the early Christians found this not in one of the gods that Romans and Greeks worshipped, but in their philosophical journeys. They found "God" not in Zeus, but in the Good of Plato, the Unmoved Mover of Aristotle, the One of Plotinus.

And they would continue that search whenever they encountered new people. Sometimes, the closest they found was some belief in a supreme deity that created all things; sometimes, it was a more abstract concept. The Jesuit missionary Mattheo Ricci (1552–1610) found "God" in the Chinese belief in "Heaven," and other similar ideas in Confucian philosophy.[11] Some efforts even led them astray; Francis Xavier (1506–52) identified the

---

9. Athenagoras, "Plea for the Christians," 6.1—7.7.

10. Acts 17:22–30. The first quote is by a Cretan philosopher Epimenides; the second is by a Cilician Stoic, Aratus.

11. Ricci's book, *The True Meaning of the Lord of Heaven* (*Tianzhu Shiyi*), which became influential in introducing Christian beliefs to Chinese, Korean, and Vietnamese literati, drew upon Confucianism in a way similar to how the early Christians drew upon Greek schools of thought such as Platonism.

Buddha Vairocana as "God," only to find too many irreconcilable differences later on.[12] Even today, the search continues. For example, Hans Küng, a Catholic theologian, compared Buddhist conceptions of Reality, or "the Absolute," with the Christian concept of "God"—and he did so even though he noted that there is no supreme being in Buddhist thought![13] Hart explains the idea of "God" to the secular readers today by drawing upon an Indian idea of *satchidananda*, or "being–consciousness–bliss," which is how Hindu philosophical schools define Reality at the ultimate level.[14]

The Christian message, "worship the one true God," was not "worship our god over your god." It was, "do not call 'God' what is *not* really 'God.'" It was, at least originally: Do not bend your knee to anything that's less than the *Infinite*, no matter how powerful or fearsome it may seem to you. You are worth nothing less than something that judges and measures even the gods. And your own traditions already taught you about this "something"—Reality, deeper than your innermost and higher than the utmost. Seek *That*. That's *Who* we profess.

"God," and not "god."

All this is certainly *not* to say that this is how Christians have always proclaimed their "God" to other people. Too many times, their proclamation was compulsion, manipulation, and denigration. And from the beginning, the Christian Gospels have issued a dire warning, in the story of the temptations of Christ, that such an approach ushers in the reign of the devil.

But we cannot tell that story yet. We're still learning its basic vocabulary. And we've only now cleared just one pile of debris; there are more.

---

12. Elisonas, "Christianity and the Daimyo," 307.
13. Küng, *Christianity and World Religions*, 378–98.
14. Hart, *Experience of God*, 42.

CHAPTER THREE

God and Science, the Universe and the Flying Spaghetti Monster

> Everything comes into being through the *Logos*.
> Without the *Logos*, not a thing comes into being.

THIS IS THE IDEA upon which our modern science is founded, an idea it inherited from Greek philosophy. And this is what it means: There are rational principles underlying everything that happens and how everything comes to be. These principles structure this reality, ordering our cosmos and shaping all life. And we can discover and describe these principles with *our* reason and language. The ancient Greeks called the unified set of these principles the "*Logos*." And in the context of modern science, this Logos encompasses all that we now call the "laws of Nature."

This is one reason why many of us today perceive our world to be God*less*. Science has enabled us to understand the world around us, and even how this entire universe came to be. Yet the world it describes has no "God," no creator entity that made it; science presents us only with this "Logos"—the principles and laws. Now, this does not prove that there is *no* such entity, no Super-Zeus-like creator in addition to these principles. But neither does it prove that there *is*. And the same can be said for alien UFOs, or even the Flying Spaghetti Monster!

This is the second debris of our Super-Zeus god we need to clear: What it means to say in our age of science that "God created the universe."

Because the quote about the Logos at the start is actually drawn *from the Bible*. From the opening lines of the Gospel of John.[1]

THE FLYING SPAGHETTI MONSTER AND CREATIONISM

Let's start with the Flying Spaghetti Monster. An invisible, undetectable pasta-entity that created the universe, according to Pastafarianism. Which is a religion for pirates today, for some reason. Yes, it's a spoof; it's a satirical critique of the idea of God held by creationists and the proponents of intelligent design. It began as an open letter to protest a school board's decision to teach intelligent design in science classes as an alternative to evolution. The letter went, if the creation story in the Bible can be taught as scientific truth, then, why not the story of the Flying Spaghetti Monster, creating the world in a drunken stupor? It'd at least be funnier.

Now, this internet meme raises a popular question: Is science in conflict with religion?

Except that that is an ill-defined question. For one thing, it's too broad. And narrowing it down to Christianity makes little difference, since this question has largely been about science and Christianity to begin with.[2] And that's only because modern science historically developed in the Christian West, so *that's where* this question was asked, for nearly two hundred years. So, let's specify our question to what the Flying Spaghetti Monster *directly* spoofs; the Christian belief that God created the world. Is there a conflict between science and *that* belief?

There are, however, at least two layers to that question.

First, is science *incompatible* with a belief that God created the universe—does science somehow disprove that belief by, for example, conflicting with the creation account in the Bible, which is presented in the book of Genesis? And the answer is: *that depends*. It'd be incompatible with one

---

1. John 1:3.

2. A good example is *The Oxford Handbook of Religion and Science*, edited by Philip Clayton, which presents an overview of the wide-ranging debate and questions regarding this topic, written by many different experts in the field. It makes a serious effort to include a broader range of perspectives, dedicating a full chapter for each of the worldviews or major religions and its relation to science, written by a representative of each viewpoint: Hinduism, Buddhism, Judaism, Christianity, Islam, and Indigenous lifeways, as well as religious naturalism, and even atheism. However, the subsequent chapters that delve into specific questions and issues regarding religion and science are still largely written within the frame of the interaction between Christianity and science.

particular way we may interpret that account—that the universe was created in six literal days with different living species appearing instantaneously rather than through the process of evolution. After all, it's this interpretation that the Flying Spaghetti Monster parodies.

But the Christian interpretation of this creation account is very diverse and complex. What we call "creation science" today, which rejects the scientific account in favor of a literal reading of Genesis, didn't even exist until the mid-twentieth century, a full century after Darwin's theory of evolution. And Christian theologians were proposing non-literal readings of the Genesis account more than sixteen hundred years before that. For example, they pointed out that according to Genesis, God did not create the sun, moon, or the stars until the *fourth day*, yet we can't have literal twenty-four-hour days without them. And Augustine, arguably the most famous among them, also pointed out that God created *time itself*. And that implies that the account of God creating the world—including how God created time—is unlikely to be a description of what God was doing *in time* or even what happened in which *chronological* order! Instead, Augustine argued that God created all things simultaneously, outside time, and the six-day narrative in Genesis was the way this truth was communicated in terms of limited, human understanding.[3]

So, understanding the Jewish and the Christian account of creation is not as simple as it may seem—let alone parody. That's why many scientists are still Christians, and why they don't see a conflict between their scientific view of the universe and their belief in God who created all things. Simply put, there are far too many ways to understand this Christian belief that are *compatible* with science—at least as many as there are ways to make them incompatible.

And that's also why *historians* of science and religion nowadays—those who've studied the history of what actually happened—largely agree that the relation between Christianity and science cannot be described simplistically as "conflict." Rather, their relationship is "*complex.*" Sometimes Christian beliefs encouraged or even directed science; sometimes they impeded and opposed it. Sometimes scientific discoveries strengthened Christian beliefs; sometimes they posed problems and puzzles; and sometimes they were just irrelevant to faith. This depended not just on specific beliefs or scientific findings, or even how those involved interpreted the Bible, but on individual circumstances, historical and cultural context, or

---

3. Augustine, *Literal Meaning of Genesis* 2.6.13; 4.26–30; 5.3–5.

even factors like which political camp you belonged to, who your camp was opposed to, and on what *your opponents* happened to believe.[4]

However, in our Godless world, it's not enough to simply say that those who believe in God don't have to hold onto views that the Flying Spaghetti Monster parodies; we don't find that a very satisfying answer. Remember: there are two layers.

To explain what I mean, let's consider one of those scientists today who do believe in God. Francis Collins is a renowned physician-scientist who headed the human genome project and the National Institutes of Health. He's an evolutionist *and* a devout Christian. And he wrote extensively on how Christianity is compatible with science, and how we can integrate both into our worldview.[5] But some atheists responded that it's not enough for Christian belief in God to be merely compatible with science; it should be *supported by it*. So, there should be scientific evidence *for* the belief that an entity like God exists. Otherwise, you're only saying that science does not *disprove* God. But, can't the same thing be said of the Flying Spaghetti Monster?

THE FLYING SPAGHETTI MONSTER AND RUSSELL'S TEAPOT

Well, can it? Let's use a slightly less exotic example as a stand-in for our Monster: The Russell's Teapot, named after Bertrand Russell, the philosopher who came up with it.[6]

Suppose you were to say that there's a teapot orbiting the Sun somewhere between the Earth and Mars. Now, we have no evidence that this teapot exists. But we have no evidence *against* it *either*. We can't prove that there's no such teapot. Does that mean that we should believe you? Of course not! That'd be ridiculous. Russell's argument was that if you believe something—like a teapot in space or the Flying Spaghetti Monster—we

---

4. This "complexity thesis" of the relation between religion and science was established by Brooke, *Science and Religion*. This thesis remains the main historiographical model today, though it continues to be refined and developed by historians. For example, see Lightman, *Rethinking History, Science, and Religion*.

5. As a scientist, Collins works within the current scientific consensus regarding cosmology and evolution. But he also believes that God created the universe, life, and human beings by directing the natural processes that science describes. See Collins, *Language of God*, 200.

6. The teapot analogy is found in Russell, "Is There a God?" 542–48.

don't need any evidence *against* your belief to say you're wrong. Rather, *you* need evidence *for* your belief. If we believe whatever we want without proof, just because there's no proof against it, we'll be swarmed by spacefaring teapots or swallowed up in the noodly tendrils of the spaghetti god! And so, likewise, even though science does not disprove our belief that God created the world, if science does not present evidence *for* that belief, it'd be like believing that there's a teapot in space.

However, there are many problems with this teapot argument. The most obvious is that Russell was wrong to say there's no evidence against his teapot. There *is*. The very reason why we think a belief in space-teapot is ridiculous is because we already know a lot of things about our world, things that *contradict* such a belief. We know what a teapot is: how it's made, its structure, composition, and fragility. And we know enough about space, and the things in it, that we know teapots don't just spontaneously form there. That means the only way for a teapot to orbit the sun is for us humans to make it and put it there. And we also know what we'd need to do to put one there, *and* that if anyone attempted it, the entire world would notice.

So, we *dis*believe Russell's teapot from the get-go, not simply because he gave us no evidence for it but also because we already have a lot of evidence *against* it. We disbelieve his space-teapot because it is *incompatible* with what we know already. What Russell failed to remember was that our beliefs don't exist in a vacuum. They are located within a large *network* of other things we believe through science, history, experience, and others. So for a belief to be compatible with the rest of the very large body of what we hold to be true is no small thing. And even the critics of Collins agree that his Christian understanding of God *is* compatible with that.

But there *is* something more noteworthy to the objection that science should support the belief in God. It's this: Granted that "God" is *not* at all like the Russell's teapot, do we still really *need* to believe in that idea? Hasn't science made our belief in an entity that created the universe unnecessary? Did it not make our entire world God*less*?

After all, the main reason why science undermined our faith in God is because it took away all the roles God had as the Creator. For example, we thought that God was the one that made the marvelous structures of each living thing. But now we know it was evolution—or the principles that dictate how life evolves. We thought that God was the one that directed the movements of the stars. But now we know it's laws of physics—of gravity and such. And we thought that God was the one that *started* everything.

But now we know that the universe began from the Big Bang. And scientists are now searching for the ultimate laws of Nature behind *that* event too. So, this line of thinking goes, science has shown that everything we once thought of as "God's work" was something else: Nature, with its principles and laws. And if science has led us to a deeper understanding of our reality *and* if there's no entity like "God" inside the reality it describes, *why should* we believe in this entity?

Now, our first chapter has pointed out the fundamental misunderstanding that lies behind this question, and I hope no one skipped that on their way here. But, here's a reminder: "God" is *not* an entity *in* Reality; God *is* Reality. So there should not be any entity that we'd call "God" *inside* the reality that science describes—for "God" points us to *reality as a whole*.

However, this only raises a new problem for us. If God is "Reality," then what does it even mean to say that "God created all things"? Does it mean anything at all in a world that is now illuminated by modern science?

It turns out that we couldn't see the answer because we were already standing on it.

THE IDEA OF THE LOGOS IS THE FOUNDATION OF SCIENCE

To understand what I mean, we'll need to take a brief detour of the historical roots of science. The very term, "scientist" didn't even exist until 1833, when the Rev. Dr. William Whewell coined it to describe what he was doing when he worked on mechanics, physics, geology, and astronomy. Yes, he was a reverend too—a Christian theologian—which was a profession that was paired with science back then much more frequently than we'd imagine today. Anyway, before this, people *we* call scientists thought of themselves as "philosophers"—or theologians, if they were feeling especially ambitious. Isaac Newton wrote on theology and his seminal work on physics was originally titled, "Mathematical Principles of *Natural Philosophy*."

So, how did philosophy become science? That's far too big a story to tell here, but we can pick up one key thread of it now: a foundational idea that science inherited from philosophy.

Centuries before Jesus was born, the ancient Greeks developed an idea that would become central to their philosophical vision. Now, they were by no means alone; philosophers of other cultures—the Indians and the Chinese, for example—developed similar ideas. And we can probably find older versions of this idea more or less everywhere. But we're talking about the Greek version, for that was the one most directly passed down to modern science.

So what was this idea? This: Rational principle governs how *everything happens* and how *everything comes to be*. And so, everything together forms not some haphazard heap but an ordered whole—a *cosmos*. That's where the word comes from; "cosmos" means "order" in Greek. And Heraclitus, one of their earliest philosophers, called this principle of order "*Logos*," a Greek word that means reason, discourse, or speech. Why did he name it "Logos"? The idea was that human "logos"—*our* reason, discourse, and speech—can somehow understand and describe the Logos *of* Reality, the principle that structures all of existence—we'll call this the "*Cosmic Logos*."[7] So, the ideal of philosophy, we could say, is to use our reason and inquiry to shape our *human* logos into the form of the *Cosmic* Logos. This, by the way, is the root idea of the word "information"; this is what we're doing, for example, when we are "being in-*formed*."

Now, the *term* changed from philosopher to philosopher; Plato and Aristotle called the rational principle "Forms" and our human capacity to reason toward it "logos." In the Roman era, the Stoics and the Neoplatonists returned to the term "Logos." But the *content* remained the same. Rational principle defines and structures everything and every happening, from the beginning to the end. And this Cosmic Logos is something *we* can understand and describe, at least to some extent, through our human logos, *our* reason and language.

Even our word, "universe," is rooted in this idea. Through the Logos, everything together forms a *unified* whole, so that everything is not only the cosmos—order—it is also the *universe*. The word comes from two Latin words, *unus*, meaning "one," and *versus*, meaning "toward." The universe is *everything* pointing us toward the *one*.

And it is upon this philosophical idea that our science was founded. Now, science has revolutionized our methods, and its precision and power

---

7. For a recent philosophical work that notably explores the significance of this idea, see Tallis, *Logos*. Raymond Tallis delves into the Gospel of John and the Genesis account of creation, as well as Greek philosophy and other ancient sources, to explore the root of this "Logos" idea in chapter 2. However, he also seems to assume that "God" refers to an *entity* in some hypothetical and unknowable "supernatural" dimension of reality—one that demeans human freedom and capability because of his exalted status. In other words, for Tallis too, "God" is a Super-Zeus, rather than the very reality we engage with at all times. I'd suggest that this is why he remains an avowed atheist, confined to the thinking habits of our Godless world.

of predictions are unparalleled. But science is *still* about informing our human logos into the form of the Cosmic Logos. The very names of our scientific disciplines remind us of this: cosmo*logy*, the logos of the cosmos; bio*logy*, the logos of life; anthropo*logy*, the logos of humanity; psycho*logy*, the logos of the mind.

IN THE BEGINNING WAS THE LOGOS, AND THE LOGOS IS GOD

Now, what's really interesting is when Jewish and Christian thinkers encountered this idea from Greek philosophy, they didn't respond by proposing an entity in addition to the *Logos*. They didn't say, "No, our god created all things, not this 'Logos.'" Nor did they say, "Some things came to be through the Logos, and God created the rest."

Instead, the Gospel of John opens by declaring that the Logos *is* God. In the English translation, "the *Logos*" is translated simply as "the Word," more or less due to a lack of better word—pun intended. Here's the original wording of the passage:

> In the beginning was the [Logos], and the [Logos] was with God, and the [Logos] was God. He was in the beginning with God. All things came into being through the [Logos], and without him, not one thing came into being.[8]

And Augustine, in recounting his lifelong journey that led him to his Christian faith, remarked that when he read the philosophical writings of the Platonists, they were teaching him these very verses from the Gospel of John, though with different wording.[9]

In our previous chapter, we explored how the Jews and the early Christians had found their "God" not in the "gods" of Greece and Rome, but in the intellectual and spiritual journey of their philosophers. The "God" that their ancestors personally encountered was less like a god and more like what these philosophers had sought—something more fundamental, the source of all things, which structures and guides the cosmos. And the *Logos* is what these Jews and Christians found and came to understand as the mind, or the "*speech*," of God.

---

8. John 1:1–3 (NRSVue). I replaced one instance of "him," with "the Logos" to highlight the usage of the term.

9. Augustine, *Confessions* 7.9.

"GOD"? WHAT'S THAT?

And this idea of the Logos *of* God is precisely how we are to understand what it means to say, "God created all things." If our reason can understand the principles and laws that structure this reality, and if our language can describe them—if our *human logos* can in some way "speak" the *Cosmic Logos*—that means Reality is *like* a rational language, a *speech*. And that brings us to the Genesis account of creation, where God *speaks*, and the world comes into being. Genesis was not describing how this world was manufactured at some distant time in the past; after all, time itself does not exist before creation. Rather, these principles, the laws of Nature—*all* of that *is* the God that speaks in Genesis. And if God did *not* speak, not a thing would exist, including time.

Now, those who see the shadow of the Flying Spaghetti Monster in God assume that "God" refers to some special entity, who is believed to have arranged the Logos—Nature and its laws—in some *very specific way*. And the believers of the Super-Zeus god agree. So, the creationists insist that our universe has chronologically unfolded in the specific order listed in Genesis 1. The proponents of intelligent design argue that the principles of evolution cannot bring forth complex life without some entity to design the specifics. The latest live issue is about whether the Logos—that is, the laws of physics—is *fine-tuned*. And science has so far found that it actually *is*. If these laws were even slightly different than they are now—if any of the physical forces were even minutely different—this universe would've been unable to form stars, or larger atoms, or would've even collapsed in on itself.[10]

But there are many things we've yet to learn about the Logos, including why it seems so "fine-tuned." Perhaps we'll discover even more fundamental principles, which can explain why these laws are exactly the way they are; perhaps the Logos is such that multiple universes are generated with different laws, and ours just has this precise set; or even perhaps our universe and its laws is a simulation that's being run in another universe. So, there are still many ways to deny that the Cosmic Logos is arranged in some special way that requires invoking this creator-entity.

Except that *none* of this is really about what Christianity means by declaring that "God created all things." Whether our universe is fine-tuned is of interest *to atheists* because it would undermine *their* worldview; for then, their world would cease to spin without some "God"—even one that's mistakenly defined as a Super-Zeus entity. And of course, that is of interest

---

10. Rees, *Just Six Numbers*, 4.

to those who want to defeat atheism. But for Christianity, if the universe is fine-tuned, its laws are the Logos of God; if there are more fundamental principles, *that* is the Logos of God; if multiple universes can be generated, *that* is the Logos of God; if it's a simulation, then it is *that, as well as the laws of the "outside" universe*, which is the Logos of God. It's not this or that specific kind of Logos, but the Logos as it is, *however it is*—that is God speaking in Genesis.

Whether it's about evolution, or chemical bonds, or gravity, or quantum fluctuations, or the Big Bang, or even multiple universes, science will *always* point us to the Logos—the principles and laws that structure all things and govern how they come to be. And science is possible only because our human logos is *like* the Cosmic Logos—because our human reason and language can understand and "speak" these principles, even if only partially. And *that* is not something science can ever do away with. And that—*that*—is God who is *speaking* all of creation into being.

This is what Albert Einstein meant when he remarked that "a conviction, akin to religious feeling, of the rationality or intelligibility of the world lies behind all scientific work of a higher order.... This firm belief, a belief bound up with deep feeling, in a superior mind that reveals itself in the world of experience, represents my conception of God."[11]

BUT IS THE LOGOS "WHO" OR "IT"?

But wait. Einstein said elsewhere that he didn't believe in the God who appears in the Bible! And this is why people find it difficult to categorize him as an atheist *or* a theist. I'd say that the idea of "God" that Einstein was fully and fervently on board with—he has religious reverence for it—is this "Logos of God." What Einstein did not believe was that this God is *personal*.

Let's look at another renowned scientist, who did identify himself clearly as an atheist. Stephen Hawking wrote in the *Brief History of Time* that "if we do discover a complete theory [on] why it is that we and the universe exist," then "we would know the mind of God."[12] He obviously meant that as a metaphor. But for Christianity, that really *is* what it would be. Because to know the mind of God is not about knowing the thoughts of some powerful entity in a higher level of reality; it is about knowing the Logos *of* Reality.

11. Einstein, "On Scientific Truth," 261.
12. Hawking, *Brief History of Time*, 191.

"GOD"? WHAT'S THAT?

Hawking seems to have become vaguely aware of this years later, when he remarked that we can think of God as the embodiment of the ultimate laws of Nature. But, he insisted that "the real crunch comes with the second question: Are there miracles, exceptions to the laws?"[13] And he then goes on to argue that there aren't. Now, his grasp of the idea of God remains shaky; he should've at least said "personification" instead of "embodiment." And his grasp of the idea of miracles is even worse, which we'll explore later. But he is right about one thing: The idea of God needs *more*; the "real crunch" comes next.

Einstein, and even Hawking, are on board with the Logos, which *is* "God" in Christianity. But, that's not enough. After all, the Bible then calls the Logos, "*Him*."

Not "*It*," but "*Him*."

And so, Augustine, after writing that philosophers taught him what was in the opening of the Gospel of John: that "all things came into being through the Logos," and "the Logos was God," confessed that they did not teach him of what followed. That the Logos became a human being and dwelt among us.[14] And this returns us to the question we raised at the end of our first chapter. How do we relate to reality? Why would we say that Reality is—that God is—*personal*? And is that even a question that science can meaningfully answer?

Here, some of us may interject, saying: Isn't it *obvious* that the Logos is *impersonal*? After all, when we say, "the Logos is God's speech," we're just using a *metaphor*—just as Hawking was using a metaphor when he referred to "the mind of God." None of this means that the principles and laws that structure our world are something that's "really" being spoken by some voice. It's like how "laws" of physics are not literally laws legislated and enforced by some cosmic power.

And all that is correct. Except that that isn't quite what Christianity is saying. Which brings us to the third debris we must clear before we can journey further: what it really means to say *any*thing about God.

---

13. Hawking and Mlodinow, *Grand Design*, 29.
14. Augustine, *Confessions* 7.9; John 1:14.

CHAPTER FOUR

Everything we say of *everything* comes with a caveat

It turns out our Godless world does not "lack" God as much as it lacks the *language* to think and speak about God. And because we who live here don't speak that language, we don't really know the words. Thus, we didn't understand *where* these words were pointing us to, so we kept looking in the wrong places. It's like they were pointing us to the sky and the stars above, and we were searching the playground, the sea-saw and the swings.

That is why we've been translating what "God" *means*, why "God" does not mean "god," and what it means to say that "God created all things." Now, let me be clear: They are by no means complete translations. But they're not wrong translations. However, we who live in this Godless world lack the knowledge of not only the *vocabulary* of this language but also its *grammar*. It's not just that we misunderstand this or that word; we misunderstand how we're to read *any* word.

Because there is a caveat to *everything* we say of God.

ISN'T WHAT WE SAY OF GOD ANTHROPOMORPHISM?

When we hear the grander pronouncements about "God," of which theologians must have penned many volumes—that "God is Being-itself, and not *a* being," or that "God is *Reality*"—we may find ourselves remembering the simpler teachings we heard. God is wise; God is strong; God is loving; God is our Father. And we can't help but feel a wide chasm between the two. It might even be that we like that simpler God *more*, even if some of us may think that such beliefs are naïve in our Godless world.

Is it really naïve though? What does it mean to say those things about God? For those things really are what Christians have believed about God. They have shaped and guided how they lived. Because the character they've attributed to God has defined how they've *related to* God—which is to say, how they've related to *reality that's all around them*.

But, this will prompt many of us to ask: isn't all of that just anthropomorphism? If God indeed is *Reality*—reality we're engaged with at all times, even at this moment—then how can we attribute *human* character to it? Isn't Reality simply beyond such characteristics? Again, if "God" is just some special entity like Super-Zeus, somewhere "out there," then maybe we can still wonder if he has qualities that *we* have. It'd be similar to how we might ask whether aliens who fly the UFOs are similar to us in anyway. Are they wise? Are they strong? Do they feel love? But how can we say that *Reality* is wise or strong or loving?

This concern underlies the accusation today that what religions like Christianity say of God are just projections; "God" is something we have *invented* by projecting our ideal human qualities, like wisdom, strength, or love, to some imaginary, external entity.[1] According to this line of thought, we've imagined that this world is ruled by some higher power, who is somehow human-like, so that it will relate to us in a personal way, with wisdom and parental love. But, our world, our reality, is *not* human; these qualities are something we've projected, perhaps because we wish that that's how reality is.

And the traditional answer from Christian theology would be surprising to many of us today. It would say that such accusations are not entirely off the mark. It *is* wrong to describe God with human characteristics. However, this does not simply mean that God is not "really" personal, or wise, or loving. Rather, these words are *inadequate*—and not just these words. There is an unspoken *caveat* to *everything* we say of God.

Now, *"caveat"* is the Latin word for "beware" or "be warned." Beware of what? That what we say about God has inherent limitations. Everything we say uses our *human* words, terms, and concepts; every personal character

---

1. This critique is exemplified by Ludwig Feuerbach's *The Essence of Christianity* (1841). His thesis in turn greatly influenced Karl Marx and Sigmund Freud, who argued that such belief in God, based on these projections, has alienated us from our true human condition and our world. See Marx, "Theses on Feuerbach"; Freud, *Future of an Illusion*.

we attribute to God are *human* characteristics. And none of that can truly describe God—describe Reality.

WE CAN'T DESCRIBE "GOD" AS HE IS; WE CAN'T NAME "REALITY" AS SUCH

Whatever we say about God is what we're saying about reality *as a whole*. That last bit is important; we're not saying something about things *inside* reality—even as a collection—but Reality *as such*. But, what can we actually say about *that*? Reality encompasses not only "everything that exists" but also "everything that does *not* exist but *can* exist," as well as *how* such things come to be and becomes whatever they are. What words could describe all of *that* "as a whole"? Other than "Being-itself," that is; except that that's not exactly a description.

And that's the idea that not only Christians but thinkers and mystics all over the world have pointed out since ancient times. Let me present just two examples from two opposite sides of the world.

The first is from the opening lines of Laozi's *Dao De Jing*, a classic philosophical text from ancient China:

> The Dao that can be described, is not the Dao as it really is,
> The name that can be said is not its name as it really is,
> Nameless is the origin of the cosmos,
> Name the mother of every particular thing,
> Always be without desire, to see their mystery,
> Always have desire, to see their manifestations,
> These two are the same,
> but they diverge with name.[2]

Now, Laozi's idea of the *Dao* has very close parallels with the idea of the *Logos* in Greek philosophy. Though the Logos literally means "discourse," and the Dao means the "Way," both ideas are about the principle that governs and guides everything that happens and how everything comes to be. In fact, the Chinese translations of the Bible usually translate the word "Logos" in the opening lines of the Gospel of John with the word "Dao."

And according to *Dao De Jing*, the Dao cannot be truly described. Words or names we use to describe the Dao are not the "unchanging Dao"—which is the literal Chinese text. Our words do not describe Reality

---

2. *Dao De Jing* 1.1–3. This is how I would translate the original text, though I have primarily referenced D. C. Lau's translation in *Tao Te Ching*.

as such; they can never grasp the Dao—the Logos—as it really is. They are inadequate. And so, "the cosmos" as a whole—"heaven and earth" in literal Chinese—has its origin in what is not named and cannot be named. Yet, we can still name how "every particular thing" *in* the cosmos comes to exist— the "ten thousand things" in literal Chinese.

That is how we speak of, and engage, *Reality*, according to Laozi.

Let me stop here, however; we'll get to the last four lines later. On the other side of the world, the ancient Hebrews were wrestling with the similar idea that we can't name God. Here's the passage from the book of Exodus in the Bible.

> Then, Moses said to God, "Suppose I go to the Israelites and say to them, 'The God of your fathers has sent me to you,' and they ask me, 'What is his name?' Then what shall I tell them?"
> God said to Moses, "I AM WHO I AM. This is what you are to say to the Israelites: 'I AM has sent me to you.'"[3]

This is a key passage in the Bible, where God's name is revealed to the Israelites. If not for this, God would've just been called "God." And this personal name of God was "Yahweh." Now, we've considered what this name means in our second chapter, and here's where it came from. The original Hebrew phrase for "I am who I am" is "*'ehye 'ašer 'ehye.*" The word, "*'ehye,*" means, "I am"; it's from the Hebrew verb, "*hayah,*" which means "*to be.*" And this verb seems to be the root-word of the name, "*Yahweh.*"

"*'Ehye*" is also an ongoing form of the verb. What do I mean by that? Well, when I say, "I ran," I've finished running. But when I say, "I'm runn*ing,*" it's still *ongoing*; I'm running now, and I'll be running for some time in the future. So, the ongoing form of this Hebrew phrase is the reason why it is translated as both "I am that I am" *and* "I will be that I will be." Except that, the verb can also mean, "I cause *to be.*" And so, the meaning of the name "Yahweh" can be "I am that I am," or "I will be that I will be," or "I cause—and *will* be causing—whatever I cause to be."

However, this name does not point us to any particular thing: no domain, no power, no role that can be attributed to a deity. God's response to Moses's request for a name instead points to something unnamable—to that undefined *anything* and *everything* that can ever happen. Simply put, it points us to "Being-itself," or "Reality" as a whole.

---

3. Exod 3:13–14.

This has led to an idea in Christianity regarding what we can and cannot say about God. The gist of it is something like this: We cannot truly describe "God" who created all things—which is to say, describe Reality *as such*, which is infinite and all-encompassing. This is because words or concepts, which describe things *inside* Reality—or in Christian terms, things that were *created*—do not apply to God. Yet, words like person, wisdom, or love, describe beings like *us*. Even words like great, or powerful, or *even existence*, describe things *inside* Reality—objects, forces, or entities—not Reality-itself; they describe things created by God, and not God.

In that sense, we can only truly say of God what God is *not*. This is called "negative" theology, which has a long tradition in Christianity, stretching back fifteen hundred years.[4]

So, does that mean whatever we say positively of God is false? If we say, for example, that God is wise or loving, are we just using anthropomorphism after all? Have we ascribed human attributes falsely to Reality? And the answer from Christianity is: *not quite*. When we are speaking about God, we need to understand that we're using analogies and metaphors.

WE HAVE TO START SOMEWHERE, SO WE USE ANALOGIES AND METAPHORS

Did you ever notice that babies keep putting things into their mouths? I mean everything; food and definitely-not food; toys and utensils and tools. It's called "baby mouthing," and one reason why they do this is because that's how they learn. It's not like they can read and write or do complex math at that point! They've yet to learn language, and the motor skills and senses for the other parts of their body, like hands, are not yet adequately developed. Their mouth, their sense of taste, is the best resource they have at that point to interact with the world around them. How things feel in their mouths, and how they taste, are what they can learn about things around them. Now, there's only so much you can learn by baby-mouthing things, but, that's where they *start*.

---

4. This idea, called "*apophatic* theology," was articulated by Pseudo-Dionysus in his *Mystical Theology*, written sometime in the fifth to sixth century, and summed up in Aquinas's preface to *ST* I.q3: "We cannot know what God is, only what He is not." Strictly speaking though, Aquinas argues that words like "being," "good," "life," apply perfectly only to God, and *we* only know them in a derived sense as they are applied to created things. See Aquinas, *ST* I.q13.a3.

"God"? What's That?

Likewise, our thinking about God has to start somewhere. And that somewhere is with words and concepts available to us, even if they are primarily about created things—things *inside* Reality. And when we use those words to describe God, they become *analogies* and *metaphors*. This is called "positive" theology.[5] They are then used together with "negative" theology, to sort of calibrate what we say about God.

Here's how it works. In negative theology, saying what God is *not* nevertheless implies something about God. But these somethings tend to be different ways of saying: "God is *not* an entity in Reality; God *is* Reality." So, for example, "God is not a being; God is Being-itself," or "God is not finite; God is the Infinite." Still, this presents us with a kind of overall framework. We then fill in the content with analogies and metaphors of positive theology. "God is *like* our father," "God is *like* a wise person," and so on. Then, we return to negative theology, which issues us a *caveat*. Be warned: We're *not* saying that God is our father in the same way humans can be fathers, or that God is wise in the same way a human person is wise.

We've already encountered several examples of how this works even in our book so far. Here's negative theology: "God does *not* exist anywhere *inside* our reality." Then, comes the analogy: "Our world is *like* a story and God is *like* an author." Then, comes the caveat: "But, there is *no outside* to God's story." Here's an example from our previous chapter, which combines the negative theology with an analogy: "God is *not* some entity that made the world; the Logos that science investigates *is* God 'speaking' in Genesis." But, be warned: the Logos of God is *like* a speech, only insofar as our speech can describe it, in some partial ways.

Here, we need to emphasize a very important point. If we think that these analogies we use to speak about God are just some "poetic way" of describing Reality and not a "real" description, we'd be *wrong*. What do I mean? Well, we tend to think this way about things like analogies and metaphors because we think there's always a "real," literal descriptions of what they're conveying. Here's an example—though it's technically a simile

---

5. The technical term is "*kataphatic* theology." For this book, we aren't going to distinguish between analogies, metaphors, and similes; for our purpose here, they are part of the same idea. The most representative articulation of the idea that everything we say about God is "analogical" is found in Aquinas, *ST* I.q13.a5–6; In contemporary theology, Sallie McFague's *Metaphorical Theology* has been influential for describing the crucial role of metaphors in describing God. For a widely read overview of Christian theology today, which discusses the role of negative and positive theology, as well as analogies and metaphors in describing God, see McGrath, *Christian Theology*, 165–70.

in this case—if I say I snuck into a room like a cat, I don't literally mean I was a cat. A security expert, or a *cat*-burglar, may be able to describe my movements more literally.

However, we tend to vastly underestimate how pervasive our metaphors and analogies are, or how they thread through the ways we speak and think about our reality in a fundamental way.[6] Even science often uses analogies and metaphors to describe things.

Take the term, the "fabric of spacetime," used by physicists. Now, we know that neither space nor time—or to be more precise, spacetime—is literally a fabric. Fabric is something we humans weave and wear. But we use the metaphor of "fabric" to describe spacetime because, according to Einstein's general theory of relativity, space and time are not simply coordinates of where and when things are; they are themselves *things*, which can bend, stretch, or contract, *like* fabric—it also gets torn quite often, if we were to believe the sci-fi movies and comic books.

Now, there's a way to describe this fabric-*like* characteristic of spacetime more literally, which is what Einstein's original papers did. But we need a special language for that based on mathematics. However, what if the only language available to us is our everyday speech? That's true at least for those of us who aren't physicists. For most of us, those equations and formulas in his papers seem no different than unreadable magic spells. We instead depend on words like "fabric" to understand his ideas.

And it turns out, many widely used scientific terms are metaphors: "black holes," "quantum waves," or even "laws" of Nature. And we use analogies extensively to characterize what science studies, such as the idea that Nature has "mechanisms," or that brain is "like a computer." Yet, these are not false descriptions of these things; we're still presented with *some* understanding of what they are. These analogies are *inadequate*, yes. But they are the best we can do with the language we have at our disposal. In fact, even scientists themselves often use analogies and metaphors to direct their research or to formulate their thought experiments.[7]

---

6. For a widely influential work on the pervasiveness of analogies and metaphors in how we understand and engage the world around us, see Lakoff and Johnson, *Metaphors We Live By*.

7. For example, Schrödinger's Cat, a well-known thought-experiment in Quantum physics, is an analogy. For an in-depth study on how metaphors and analogies play a significant role in the actual practice of scientific inquiry, see Wuppuluri and Grayling, *Metaphors and Analogies in Science and Humanities*.

Then, what if we are trying to describe something that no existing human language—no possible language—can truly describe? We'd use analogies. And we'd use them with a caveat. Everything positive we say of God is analogical in that sense. They are the best we can say with the words and language available to us human beings; after all, what's the alternative?

HOW CAN ANALOGIES REALLY DESCRIBE REALITY?

But, how can we possibly speak *true* analogies about God? After all, analogies in sciences are true, because there's a more accurate description of reality—those equations and formulas that they're based on. How can an analogy be true if that's the only thing we got?

To answer, we first need to remember that our analogies about God are *not* about an entity in some inaccessible, higher level of reality. Then, we'd indeed have no way of knowing if these analogies are true in any sense. But, God *is Reality*. So, what we say about God is what we're saying about the very reality we're engaged with even now. Analogies about God thus describe what we actually *experience*—everything and every possible thing, at the widest possible scale.

And it turns out, as we try to describe the world around us on a wider and wider scale, we tend to rely more and more on *some* sort of analogies or metaphors. For example, regarding our physical universe, we've invoked the analogies of "machine," or "laws," or even "dice." And even this is not the widest scale, because Reality is *more* than the universe.

At the widest scale, we all rely on analogies to characterize reality "as a whole." And that means our question at the end of our first chapter—whether Reality is a Who or a What—is actually a *question of analogies*. And it's a comparative question: Which set of analogies seems to be the *best*? To characterize all of reality *and* to guide how we relate to It—or "Him"? And the Christian idea of "God" is a candidate for just such a set.

So, what kind of analogies should we expect to find there?

First, think about the idea that the principles and laws that structure the universe is the God that "speaks" in Genesis. The analogy is that, at the widest scale, reality is *like* a speech, because our speech can describe its principles; that's how our reality seems to be structured. Here's another: reality is *like* a story. The history of the universe—well, the history of *anything*—is a story; we can't seem to describe how it unfolds without telling *some* kind of story. So, "story" does seem to characterize *what* history is.

Now of course, neither analogy quite gets us to the idea that God is the "speaker" or the "author." But that's for the next chapter.

But not every analogy about God is some generalized observation about reality like this. Many more are from "revelation." And according to Christianity, these are particular things that people in the Bible *discovered* about God. Discovered, in the sense that you may discover that your friend volunteers at a shelter, or that your mother treasures that photo of you taking the first step, or that your father was actually Santa Claus. These are things you find out from particular events and experiences—and you find out because you were *meant* to. That is, your friend, your mother, or your father, "revealed" them to you.

What does it mean though for there to be analogies about God—analogies that characterize our reality—from what is "revealed"? And this returns us to the opening lines of *Dao De Jing*, as well as the book of Exodus.

According to Laozi, names we use to describe things depend on how they *relate to us*—that is, what they are to us, in terms of what we're *doing*. Here's the latter part of the quote used earlier: "Always be without desire, to see their mystery; Always have desire, to see their manifestations." And this is what it means. Our "desire" defines our purpose, and our purpose defines our actions. And our actions—or *inter*actions—with something defines *what* that thing is *to us*.

Take the seat you're sitting on. Why is that a seat? It could be described as a lump of matter, or whatever it's made out of. Maybe it's not even a proper chair, but a tree stump, or a cushion, or a table. Hopefully, it's not something even more exotic, like an animal, or a person. Why a seat? Because of its relation to you: You're *sitting on it*.

There's always *more* to things than how they relate to us and what we're doing; that's why "without desire," we'll "see their mystery." But, how something relates to us is the basis of the words we use to name it. Is it "soil" for your potted plant? Or is it a "sample" of mineral, gases, organic matter, and organisms? Or is it the "mud" you need to clean up after your dog played outside and ran in?

And this is true of *personal* relationships, though in their case, it's more bi-directional: what *they* are doing, as well as what you are doing. What makes someone your "mother"? Having given you birth? What about how she raised you? Her influence over you? How you've acted around her? What would make a biological mother *not* your "mother"?

Then, what about *Reality*? What about God?

"God"? What's That?

In the Exodus passage, God declares that God's name, "Yahweh," means "I am that I am" and "I will be that I will be." Yet in the same passage, just before pronouncing that name, God also declared to Moses: *"I will be with you,"* using the exact same verb, "to *be*," in the exact same ongoing form (*'ehyeh*). And God "will be" *with* Moses so that his fellow Israelites will be freed from their enslavement in Egypt and return here with him.[8]

Again, "I will be that I will be" points to something unnamable and infinite—Reality, which can unfold anything and everything. But, there is another aspect to this name of God. This "I will be" also "will be with" Moses, so that he will find out *Who* God is *to* him, by experiencing what reality will now unfold in his life.

And what unfolded as Reality and Moses engaged each other would become the basis for more concrete "names" of God. For near the end of the Exodus story, after God frees the Israelites from Egypt, Moses again hears God speaking. On the mountain where God once declared, "I am that I am," God now declares:

> "[Yahweh], [Yahweh], the compassionate and gracious God, slow to anger, abounding in love and faithfulness, maintaining love to thousands, and forgiving wickedness, rebellion and sin. Yet he does not leave the guilty unpunished."[9]

These were human traits. God is—Reality is—beyond such traits, but these were the analogies that nevertheless characterized the reality that Moses *experienced* in his journey. And again, such characterizations are true in a comparative sense; they are *better* than others. "Compassion," "grace," "love and faithfulness," but also "justice," turned out to be the *best* human words available to him that described what he experienced—Reality that unfolded freedom for his people.

As to what it means to actually experience something like that, that's what we're hoping to explore.

---

8. Exod 3:12.

9. Exod 34:6–7a (NIV). Again, "Yahweh" is written as "LORD" in English Bible translations. In this book, whenever the quoted text uses that translation, we will return to the name, "Yahweh" to recall for us its *meaning*.

PART TWO

What do you mean God "speaks"?

CHAPTER FIVE

What do you mean God "speaks"?

CHRISTIANITY IS FOUNDED ON the idea that God speaks, and that we can hear him. That we can speak with God is central to the belief that Reality is a *Who*, not a *What*.

But, what does it really mean to say that God "speaks"?

Let's take an example of someone in the Bible "hearing" God speaking to them, say from a burning bush. Such events are obviously profound and life-changing—history-changing even. But those of us who live in a Godless world often find it difficult to imagine, let alone understand, what could've happened. Did they hear an audible voice—literal, physical sound waves in the air? But where did *that* come from? From the sky? Or the bush? And how *loud*? Was it a booming voice? Or a mysterious voice with an odd ring to it? Or perhaps, it was a voice or a vision in their heads. But how is that different from a hallucination or a psychotic episode? And in trying to imagine what happened, we'd likely imagine something that's not too different from a scene in a sci-fi movie, when some alien being makes a psychic link with someone. We understand "God speaking" as some *entity*, making contact with us from somewhere "out there."

But, what does it mean to say that God "speaks" if God is not a mere entity in our reality, but the whole of reality we're engaged with, even now, and at all times? Then we'd need to rethink *everything* about what it means for God to "speak" and for us to "hear."

"SPEAKING" IS WHAT MAKES GOD "GOD" TO THOSE WHO "HEAR"

Everything we say concretely of God is an analogy or metaphor. For we all draw on analogies and metaphors to characterize our reality at the widest scale. And what the Christian idea of "God" presents is a candidate for the best set. Yet an analogy is more appropriate, or less, depending on *how* it is being used. So, "God" is in a sense *like* a god; we relate to God in personal ways; God "speaks" and "acts" in our lives; we respond with awe and reverence. But beware: "God" of theistic traditions like Christianity is *not* a "god" like Zeus, nor some super-version of such gods. God is *Reality*.

Or rather, that's the translation; "Reality" is what we who live in a Godless world would call "God."

However, this likely conjures yet another metaphor—or analogy—for our minds today. God is like an *infinite ocean*, so that "we live, move, and have our being" *in* this "God." Maybe we imagine an endless sea of light. Perhaps we give it an appropriately mysterious name like "Force," or "Spirit." If our previous analogy was from ancient myths, this analogy is from the Star Wars movies—that of some universal Force. And this too *is* appropriate to some extent; after all, God *is* "Being-itself, not a being," and "the infinite ocean of being that gives existence to all reality." Except of course, every analogy has its limits—no exceptions.

Oceans *don't speak*.

Jedis can feel the Force and sense its ebb and flow. But the Force doesn't exactly initiate a conversation—and Force ghosts don't count; they're just spirits of dead Jedis. And when we really think about it, even an ocean, or the Force, is *still an entity*, just like Super-Zeus; it's still something *inside* Reality—it's just more diffuse and spread out.

God is Reality. And Reality "speaks." *That* is the idea of God.

But *does* God speak? And what does it *mean* for God to "speak"? Even as an analogy? What does it mean for *reality* that's all around us, reality with which we're always engaged with, to "speak to us"?

And it turns out that this question is not so much about God, but about *us*. Here's what I mean. When we ask what it means for God to "speak," we're also asking what it means for us to "hear." How do *we* "hear" God speaking? And how do we know *that* God is speaking?

And we tend to answer by pointing at *examples* of people hearing God or at least some god or other—though again, "God" is not "god." So, Homer called upon a goddess to recite his epic of the *Iliad* and Confucius declared

What do you mean God "speaks"?

that at fifty, he heard the will of Heaven.[1] In the Bible, God, whose name is "I am that I am," spoke to Moses from the burning bush and told him to go and free his fellow Israelites from their enslavement in Egypt. Today, people hike to commune with Nature, or meditate to encounter their spirit guides, while Christians close their reading of the Bible with the words, "This is the word of the Lord."

But, these are examples. In fact, we don't even know whether any of these examples are legitimate in the first place. After all, they don't tell us *why* these things are "hearing" God speak. What do they mean when they say that God spoke to them? How did they "hear" these words? And how can we know that what they heard were in fact *God* "speaking"? How can we know when these are *not*?

First, the obvious: Hearing God speak isn't necessarily about physically hearing audible words—I'd still add that it *can* be, but let's leave that alone. People who hear from God often report that it's hearing "from the heart," or the "inner voice in our mind." But that's not too helpful either since we have *many* thoughts, many feelings, many inclinations, going on in our hearts and minds. So the real question is: Why would we think that *one of those* is God speaking to us?

On the other hand, Christians say that God speaks to us through their Bible—but again, why should we think that? What about *other* books? And if we do believe that God speaks through the Bible, the Bible still says many things, and people sometimes disagree about what it's really saying. So, how do we know what God is saying at any particular point in our lives?

Imagine that you asked me what a *"sound"* is, and I answered by turning on the radio and showing you how to make it louder or softer. Then later, I banged on a drum and hummed a tune. If you didn't already know what a "sound" was, I would've only confused you. Answering by just pointing to examples isn't very helpful unless we already understand why those examples are, well, *examples*.

So for now, let's leave the examples—the Bible, or even how God speaks personally *to* people, whether audibly, or in their hearts, or otherwise. We'll instead focus on just our first question.

What does "God speaks" mean?

---

1. *Iliad* 1.1–7; *Analects* 2.4.

"GOD"? WHAT'S THAT?

TRUTH IS "HEARING" GOD "SPEAK"

To put it in simplest terms, *Truth* is God speaking.

We've actually skipped a crucial step, but we'll start here. Truth is what God "speaks." And I don't just mean that everything God says is true; that'd just mean that God is a special entity that knows everything and does not lie. I mean that *every truth* is God speaking—and yes, this "speaking" is again an analogy. And I should note here that in Christianity "truth" is linked with "goodness" and "beauty," so that a search for truth also invokes the search for the other two. But here, we'll focus on truth.

Now, there's a Christian dictum that states, "All truth is God's truth." It condenses two thousand years of Christian thinking and writing. The apostle Paul wrote in his letter to the Romans that all peoples know some truth about God, though they've failed to honor this God they know *as* God. A few centuries later, Augustine reminded his readers that truth, wherever it's found—even in pagan sources—is from God. Similar position was affirmed in the medieval era, with Thomas Aquinas stating that God is "Truth-itself." It continued during the Protestant Reformation as John Calvin warned that to reject truth from profane authors outside the Christian faith is to insult the fountain of all truth, which is the Spirit of God.[2]

The implication of this age-old dictum is two-fold. First, Christians are to recognize and affirm truth *wherever* it's found, whether it's from the sciences, literature, or the arts, from other religions or philosophies, and even when it's from horrific people! They must take pains to search for such truth even if it's jumbled and fused with mistakes or misconceptions, or even outright lies. And second, not only should they affirm these truths, they must acknowledge that these truths are from none other than God!

Thus, every truth, in a sense, is God speaking. And that means, whatever truth that *you* hold—if it really is true—*is* what *God* is speaking, at least on that matter.

Now, this rather mundane definition seems to pose some strange implications. For example, even things like "2+2=4," or "squirrels dig holes in the ground to hide their food," would be something God is speaking. But, imagine a scene in the Bible where God calls to someone from a burning bush, only to say, "squirrels dig holes in the ground"!

---

2. Rom 1:18–22; Augustine, *On Christian Doctrine* 2.18; *ST* I.q16.a5; Calvin, *Institutes of the Christian Religion*, 2.2.15.

However, that's not quite what this means. First, not everything God is speaking is something God is speaking *to* us. More importantly, we skipped a crucial step by simply saying "Truth is God speaking." What we call "truth" is not God speaking per se; it is us, *hearing* what God is speaking.

What's the difference? Well, the classical definition of truth is that truth is about the *relation* between our thoughts regarding something and what that something really is.[3] For example, if I think that a squirrel dug holes in my garden last night, what I think is *true* if and only if a squirrel really dug holes in my garden last night. So, in the broadest sense, truth is about the relation between our thoughts and reality—it's about how our engagement *with* reality "adequately" informs what we believe.[4]

And this returns us to the idea that *our* logos can understand and speak the *Cosmic* Logos. That is what it means to "hear" God speak. "Truth" is what we can learn—that is, "hear"—as we engage reality.

And *reality* is what God is "*speaking*."

ALL OF REALITY IS "GOD SPEAKING"

Reality is speech-*like*. We can understand and meaningfully *speak* about its structures, its principles and patterns; we can *narrate* how it has unfolded through time. That's what we are "hearing" though science and history. The principles and laws that define how everything comes to be is God "speaking" in Genesis; the entire history of the world is God "speaking" to

---

[3]. This is summed up in the formula, "truth is the adequacy of things and the intellect" (*veritas est adaequatio rei et intellectus*) in Aquinas, *ST* I.q16.a1; see also *ST* I.q16. aa2–3. According to Aquinas, the formula itself is from a ninth-century Jewish Neoplatonist, Isaac Israeli, but the general definition of truth as a relation between our intellect and things is from Aristotle and Plato.

[4]. I'd caution those who are familiar with the contemporary philosophical debate about "truth," that this position is *not* quite what they know as the "correspondence theory of truth" today. Philosophers since the modern era have tended to conceive "correspondence" in terms of how our mental representations mechanically "mirror" the things in the "outside world." And this theory is beset with the problem of *how* and even *whether* such mirroring can be done, which is the sustained critique that Richard Rorty leveled against it in his *Philosophy and the Mirror of Nature*. However, the classic definition that "truth is the adequacy of things and the intellect" is something much broader; I'd even suggest that this "adequacy" can be defined to encompass not only "correspondence" in the contemporary sense, but the "coherentist," "pragmatist," and even "constructivist" theories in some way. After all, it only requires that our reason and intellect can meaningfully engage reality in *some* way, so that our thoughts are in*formed* by this engagement.

unfold it. That is why *all* truth is God's truth. Every truth we learn, every truth we say, is from our engagement with reality, and *reality* is what God is "speaking."

If this way of thinking about God sounds strange to us, this is largely due to how we've misunderstood the relation between God and the world. And it's closely knit with how we've imagined God to be some "Super-Zeus" entity. Again, everything we say of God is an analogy. And the dominant analogy for God's relation to the world as its creator, since the modern era, has been that of an engineer and a machine. And this analogy seemed true when people first came up with it; Nature did seem *like* a machine, so God did seem like a kind of engineer who designed and made this machine. But this analogy was *fraught* with problems.

Again, the Christian idea of God is that all things not only came into existence by God's power, but they *continue to exist by that same power*. But a machine runs on its own once it's assembled and turned on; it continues to exist without its maker. Furthermore, in Christianity, because things continue to exist by God's power, God is understood to be present *in* all of creation. So in a sense, to perceive the universe *is* to perceive God. But, when we see a machine, we don't see its maker; we can only infer that there was someone who made it.

So, in the machine-and-engineer analogy, the universe is an *artifact* that was "assembled," "turned on," and then "left behind," and we are now speculating who left it behind and why.[5] The question about the Creator then becomes "what is the purpose of this artifact?" This, in turn, leads us to ask if the mechanical design of the universe is *efficient* in fulfilling this hypothetical purpose. And if not, we'll question whether this machine was really designed by some intelligent being. So, with this analogy, "God" becomes some hypothetical alien engineer, nowhere to be found around the machine before us.

And it turns out that "machine" was not a good analogy for Nature either. Now, some of us may ask why not? Isn't it a good analogy, at least for the physical universe—especially if you are a materialist?

But contemporary physics has pushed our understanding of "matter" far beyond this imagery of a "machine." We used to think that all matter is made up of tiny particles called "atoms." Then, we found that atoms are made up of even smaller particles, which in turn are made up of even

---

5. This lies at the heart of how naturalistic view of science misunderstands the idea of God and the doctrine of creation. See Hanby, *No God, No Science?*, 3–4, 120–29.

smaller ones, until we found that matter is made up of "fields"—intangible, formless, and defined only in terms of abstract mathematics. Moreover, according to scientists like Hawking, the entire physical universe—or the multiverse, *if* that exists—came into being through some "ultimate laws of physics." And "laws" are *not* some *material* thing; it's more like codes, algorithms, or *information*.[6] So, everything we're now saying about matter, or the physical universe, is pointing not to a machine but back to the idea of the *Logos*.

It's actually a popular misconception that science "proves" that our universe is physical. Science cannot actually confirm—let alone "prove"— such a thing. Here's an example. There's a proposal going around today that this world may actually be some kind of computer simulation.[7] If so, what we thought was a "physical" universe would really be just *software*—codes and data. Now, I do not believe that we're living in a simulation, and even if we were, both this "simulated world," and the "outside world" would be God's "story." My point though is that unless the simulation itself somehow "glitches," nothing that science can discover about our "physical" universe can disprove this thesis; science cannot tell us whether this universe is actually physical, or is just codes and data. That's because what science "proves" is *not* that the world is physical—that's simply assumed—but what principles define its structures. And perhaps these principles are just codes of a program; or perhaps they really are physical laws. Either way, science is about these principles; it's about the *Logos*.

So, what truly characterizes our reality is that it is speech-*like*. It *may* be physical; it *may* be simulation; but it *is* speech-like. Reality is like a "speech" in the broadest sense, in that speech *communicates*. That is why science can describe Nature; why we can discuss justice; why poetry can be beautiful. Of course, there are things about reality that are beyond mere words, but there are means to communicate, which are beyond words—for example, mathematics, or music.

Reality communicates; that is its *fundamental character*.

And *that* is what it means to say that God "speaks." The analogy is that everything is *like* a speech, so that this world, its principles and laws, and its entire history, is something that God is spea*king*. And this "speaking" is ongoing, just like how God's declaration that "I am that I am" is an ongoing

---

6. The most explicit and controversial version of this idea, among scientists, is the concept of "It from Bit" in John Wheeler's paper, "Information, Physics, Quantum."

7. Bostrom, "Are You Living in a Computer Simulation?"

form of "to *be*." That's why everything not only comes to exist, but *continues to exist*, by God's power. Everything—the universe, life, ourselves, every entity and every event—is something that is even now "be*ing* spoken."

The initial translation of "God" for our Godless world was that "God" is "*Reality*." But the translation was incomplete, a starting sketch. Now, we can refine it further.

All of *reality* is "God *speaking*."

WHAT DO YOU MEAN GOD IS THE "SPEAKER"?

Those of us whose thinking habits were hardened in our Godless world may now raise this following point: The speech-like character of our reality does not mean that there has to be some sort of "speaker"! And I'd agree. However, I'd first ask whether we've slid back into thinking of God as some Super-Zeus entity, who is speaking our reality from somewhere "outside" it. Then, we'd have forgotten the limit of our analogy from the first chapter; God is *like* an author of a story, but there is no outside to God's "story." Likewise, all of reality is God speaking, and by definition, there can be no outside to *all* of reality.

But then, what would it even mean for God to be the "Speaker"?

Now, the analogy of God as the Speaker poses a radical difference from that of God as an engineer of a machine. When we hear a speech, we don't *infer* a speaker—to hear the speech *is* to hear the speaker; the speech and the speaker is a single package, so to speak. So then, here's a question: In everyday life, why do we distinguish speakers from what they speak?

And there are two key reasons why. The first is the most obvious: We exist "outside" of what we speak. Our bodies physically exist separately from the sounds we make when we utter words. But, this first reason cannot apply to God, because there is no outside to God speaking—no outside realm, or outer reality, *in which* God is speaking our world; because again, *all* of reality is God speaking.

But there's a second, equally significant reason. Speakers can say things *other than* what was spoken. For example, I'm speaking this very sentence aloud right now; but I could've spoken something else instead, or sang a song, or even stayed silent. And of course, I've spoken many, many other things in my life. And speakers can also speak something in the future that's entirely different than what they spoke so far. Or to use an analogy of an author and a story, authors can tell a different story than what they told; Shakespeare wrote *Hamlet*, but he could've written something else, or

What do you mean God "speaks"?

chosen not to write it, and of course, he has written many other stories, like *King Lear, Othello, Romeo and Juliet,* before and after writing *Hamlet.*

Likewise, to say that our reality is not just speech-like but *is* "God speaking" is to say that there's a myriad of other speech-like realities that could have been "spoken" instead. We could've lived different lives, experienced different things, met different people. The history of our nations could've been different, so that the U.S. never declared independence. The course of evolution could've been different, so that dinosaurs evolved into sentient beings instead of us humans. The universe as a whole could've been different; in fact, that's the idea of the multiverse—that there may be other versions of the universe where not only different things happened, or different things exist, but which are governed by different laws of physics altogether. Or, our reality could've even been *nothing at all.*[8] So, our analogy is that reality is *like* something that was spoken forth, instead of infinite others that could've been spoken, or even simple *silence.*

Our reality can also unfold new things—things that never existed before, things we've never imagined. That is why Reality is more than the sum of everything that exists; it encompasses an infinite array of possibilities. So, again our reality is not just "speech-like," but like something that is even now be*ing* spoken forth, unfolding *new* things, making mere possibilities into real things—a "Speaker" that is even now continuing to speak.

And this introduces some distinctions within our initial translation that "God" is "Reality." There is our speech-like reality—everything and every happening—which is God "speaking." But, this *everything* is just one way things have unfolded so far; it could've unfolded differently, and it still can. And so, at the most fundamental level, "Reality" is the *Infinite,* and this is "God" who could have and still can "speak" infinite other speech-like realities. And there's no clear answer as to why *this* reality is being spoken. But if Reality is a *Who*—if God is the "Speaker"—then perhaps the answer is something that's analogous to why *we* decide to speak something: our will, or purpose, or even love.

The Infinite; the act of "speaking" our reality; and the Will: These three loosely correspond to the Christian idea of the Trinity—God as Three in

---

8. In philosophy, this raises the question, "why there is something rather than nothing?," which leads to what is called the cosmological argument for God. However, "God" we're exploring here is not simply some answer to this question, but the very reality that we're experiencing now—our speech-like reality, which could've been different, or again, even empty.

One. The Father who "created all things"; the Son who is "the Logos of God"; and the Holy Spirit who reveals to us what God "wills."[9]

But, don't get too tied up with this analogy; for one thing, it's missing the intensely personal nature of the relationship between the Father, Son, and the Spirit. And we can't even begin to explore that idea without going through the entire journey of the Christian Bible—and this book can only take us to the starting line.

FROM GOD "SPEAKS" TO GOD "SPEAKS TO US"

The phrase "God speaks" is pointing to something far, far wider than what we've imagined: the infinite, speech-like reality. So, when we engage reality, and everything that is unfolding, we are "hearing" what is "be*ing* spoken." And we can only hear a tiniest fraction. There are, no doubt, things that God is speaking now, things in some unreachable corner of reality, that we will *never* hear. But the part we do hear, and hear "adequately," in whatever way, is "truth." That's what it means for us to "hear" God "speak" in the broadest sense.

We may wonder though how we can ever go from something so *im*personal to the deeply personal God of the Bible who speaks with people. Because the analogies about reality that we've explored so far—that all of reality is God "speaking," or even that God is the "Speaker"—do not quite get us to God who personally converses with us. But that's to be expected. Because what reveals the God that speaks as *Who* rather than *What* is the *content* of what is spoken *to* us. And we have not yet explored what that means.

However, we needed to start here, because if we didn't, we'd be working with a fragmented understanding of what it means for God to "speak." And that would in turn mislead us into asking all the wrong questions when we try to understand what it means for God to speak "*to us*." We've now set the foundation, a definition, to which we can *measure* the claims about hearing from God.

---

9. Those who are familiar with Christian theology may note some similarity with Augustine's psychological analogy of the Trinity, of memory, understanding, and will or love. See Augustine, *On the Trinity*, 14.6, 8, 10. And in fact, it is precisely this kind of trinitarian relation to creation, which was lost in the analogy of God as engineer of a machine-artifact. See Hanby, *No God, No Science?*, 121.

What do you mean God "speaks"?

To hear God speak is to hear *truth*. People may claim that God spoke to them; they may point to their status in religion or society; they may appeal to our feelings or passions; they may even quote the Bible. But, the primary marker for hearing God speaking is *truth*, and what all that means. And I don't just mean factual truths. There are truths about what is right and wrong, truths about what is meaningful; truths about what Reality—what "*Yahweh*"—is *unfolding*. So, in the Bible, Moses heard from God these following words:

> You may say to yourselves, "How can we know when a message has not been spoken by [Yahweh]?" If what a prophet proclaims in the name of [Yahweh] does not take place or come true, that is a message [Yahweh] has not spoken.[10]

That is the measure, specified in the Jewish and the Christian Bible, of what it means to have heard from God.

This, however, confronts us with more questions. What then is the difference between "hearing God speak" and "hearing God speak *to us*"? And *can* we ever really know the "truth" in a world where our truth seems to be constantly changing, too often propped up by power and selfish interests? In fact, shouldn't we be suspicious of anything that says this is the *whole* truth—some perfect grasp of *Reality*? And where does the Bible fit into all of this for Christianity?

For we still have a long journey ahead to explore what it means to say, "God speaks."

---

10. Deut 18:21–22 (NIV).

CHAPTER SIX

What do you mean God "*speaks to* you"?

"Now God spoke to Abram, 'Go from your country and . . . .'"

Wait. Wait. Hold up. Hold up. What do you mean, God *spoke*? And what's hearing from God supposed to be like anyway?

That was my first reaction many years ago when I read the opening of Abraham's life-story in the Bible—when I *really* read it. It starts by simply stating that God spoke to a man named Abram. It reported this as if this was something completely routine—no different from a father speaking to his child during breakfast about an upcoming family trip.

There were other stories where there was something more to God speaking to people. Jacob had a dream of a ladder that stretched from earth to the sky; Moses heard God from a burning bush; Isaiah saw a vision of God as he worshipped in the temple; Paul and his companions, on their way to arrest Christians in a faraway city, was struck by light, though only Paul heard a voice speak to him. But, there were many other times when the Bible simply stated that God spoke to a person. What actually happened there? How did they know that God spoke to them? And even the examples with dreams or visions or lights did not answer the question: Why is *that* something God was speaking to them?

All of reality is "God speaking." But, there's a difference between "God speaking," and "God speaking *to you*." And in the Bible, God speaks *to* people.

So, what does that mean?

WHAT DO YOU MEAN GOD "SPEAKS TO YOU"?

THE QUESTION OF WHAT IT MEANS TO SAY "GOD SPEAKS TO US"

It's vitally important to understand that the Christian idea of "God who speaks" is infinitely wider than our popular imagination of some entity coming into contact with people to convey some special message. Rather, our entire reality is speech-*like*—something God is "speaking." And every truth we reach from our engagement with this reality is "hearing" what is "being spoken"—and not just factual truth, but truths about what is good and what gives our life beauty and meaning. That's what it means, in the broadest sense, to say that "God speaks."

But, saying that "God speaks *to* us," is more than that. We can compare this to how *people* can speak to us. For example, we may hear someone speak on a radio or a podcast, but they're not really speaking *to* us. Now, sometimes, they may say something that really "speaks to us." But what we mean is that they said something that we found meaningful. It resonated with us because it was describing the kind of things we experienced or was answering the questions we're struggling with. These speakers were not speaking *to* us in the sense that they were interacting with us in a personal way. They spoke and we heard, but we did not have a conversation; we haven't spoken back to them, and they wouldn't have replied even if we had.

According to Christianity, God speaks, *and* God speaks *to* people. That is why Reality is *Who*, not What. This is the point where those of us who believe in God, and those of us who don't, truly part ways—the real reason why one side calls Reality "God" and the other does not. So, what does it mean for "Reality" to speak *to* us *personally*?

And at this point, we may think of "religious experiences." Surely, any personal encounter with God is some sort of religious experience? And that may be true. But exploring our question in terms of religious experiences would pose some significant problems for us.

First, "religious experience" is bewilderingly diverse and varied. For example, *Varieties of Religious Experience*, a modern classic on this subject from 1902 by William James, lists ecstasies and rapture, feelings of sin and despair, sense of peace and forgiveness, conversions, saintliness, and mystical experiences. And we now know there are many, many more mediated through rituals and practices of different religious traditions: what we experience as we pray, meditate, sing hymns, read scriptures, or participate in communal worship. So, which one is God speaking *to* us? All of it? Some of it? And why? We've expanded our question far beyond the scope of what we can explore here.

The second problem is that we tend to view "religious experiences" as something special and *rare*. We tend to imagine them to be somehow highlighted with some special qualities—a sense of certainty, or awe, or mystery, which will feel like some divine stamp of authentication.[1] And of course, such experiences may indeed be examples of God "speaking to us." But again, *which ones*? And why? More importantly, though there are many examples in the Bible where experiences of God speaking to people have such special qualities, there are also many that don't. Often in the Bible, God simply just speaks to people—like how we'd just start a conversation. No blinding light, no awe-inspiring encounters or visions, no fire, thunder, and earthquakes, but just a small, still voice.[2]

For Christianity, God speaking *to us* points to something much wider, which has to do with how we *relate to* God—to reality as a whole. That does include rare, awe-inspiring, transformative experiences. But those are just a part of something larger. God speaking to us is an ongoing, life-long conversation that unfolds throughout our entire lives. It's about how what we do, and the way we live, is guided and led by God through many different means.[3]

However, this leads us to our third problem. It is this "ongoing conversation with God" that we're trying to *translate* for our God*less* world. And a world that does not really understand what "God" points to has no point of reference to understand what an "ongoing conversation with God" would mean. So, if we want to continue, we really have only two options. We can take the plunge and start living among those who are actually living this kind of life, and sort of imitate their example, then see what happens. Or,

---

1. For example, according to James, mystical experiences are characterized by ineffability, noetic knowledge, transience, and passivity. See James, *Varieties of Religious Experience*, 380–81. A decade later, Rudolf Otto introduced the idea of the *"numinous"* experience as what characterizes the biblical encounter with God. This is the experience of something "wholly other," an ineffable mystery that is both terrifying and fascinating. See Otto, *Idea of the Holy*, chapters 5–6.

2. 1 Kgs 19:9–18. However, this idea of a small, still voice threads throughout what Christianity has called an "indwelling of the Holy Spirit," which is the teaching that the Spirit of God speaks from within as a gentle guide and teacher to those who believe in Christ.

3. This point is emphasized in a Dallas Williard's *Hearing God*, 11–13, 29–30. Williard also suggests in chapter 5 that a "still, small voice" seems to be the most prominent way that God speaks to humanity.

we can do that, *but* start with some rough and ready translation. I'm afraid there's no option that leaves out having to "live it out" at some point.

But, what rough and ready translation can we start with? If "God" *is* "Reality," and all of our speech-like reality is God "speaking," then what would a *personal* and ongoing conversation with "Reality" be? How can we *begin* to understand that, starting from a Godless world?

Perhaps we can start with this.

There is, in each of us, a voice that speaks our most truthful thoughts.

THERE ARE "INNER" VOICES THAT SPEAK TO US AND SHAPE OUR LIVES

To be precise, there are many voices that speak within each of us. These voices contend with each other in the arena of our minds. And no, I don't mean hearing voices or people that aren't there. What I mean is that whenever we're faced with decisions, whether large, life-changing ones, or small, forgettable ones, there's a debate inside us. And there are "sides" to that debate; we may not perceive them as distinct "voices" that literally speak to us, but each presents a path to take. Each *communicates* a choice.

Throughout our life, we are often pulled in multiple directions, because there are different sides of us that are competing against one another regarding our decisions. You have that work that you need to finish by tomorrow? But, there's a part of you that says, let's just go out, and do it in the evening; another that says, we need to complete the job now. Then, perhaps another that reminds you there's something even more important, like reconciling with a friend you've hurt.

And these different voices can compete on truly life-changing things. Should you quit your unfulfilling job and pursue your passion, say, of making a film? One voice fumes at how you were again passed over for promotion and says you should quit. Another says you are naively abandoning your financial security for something you're not ready for. Yet another says you only live once, and you should only do things you want to do, while another fearfully throws up image after image of failure. Something also seethes, about how your family doesn't support your dreams, how you're overlooked at your job, and how your life seems worthless. Then, there's a voice, which is quietly asking you whether all this is truly about your passion, or your desire to hide from your current fears and failures.

We may also notice that some significant voices seem consistent across time. They represent vague, but distinct personalities. There's the aggressive one that tells you to hit back hard and fast; the ponderous one that urges you to be patient and not make rash decisions; the hedonistic one that tells you to live it up and ignore the consequences; the fearful one that tells you no risk is worth taking; the dark, spiteful one that rears its head when things are going bad, wanting you to curse at everything and everyone, including yourself.

And these personalities do not suggest; they demand. They may not demand with actual words; it may be a sentiment, or pure impulse, or feeling. But they are there, standing in your psychic space, posing a possible way of living for you to follow.

But, which of these should you follow? Because you will be going down the path that one of these voices is speaking, and that will in turn shape your life and your world around you. And you want to listen to the voice that's telling the truth—one that's not making a mistake or lying to you. After all, we can also lie to ourselves.

And that's how we tend to regard these voices today; they are just different sides of *ourselves*. We identify them as representations of our different values, motivations, or impulses. But, psychologically, we rarely experience these voices as some abstract statements of values or motivations. We encounter them as personalities that pose feelings or attitudes or thoughts—personalities we ourselves manifest when we follow them. Only afterward do we articulate these experiences into abstract principles, like "aggression," or "prudence," or "hedonism," or "fear," or "spite."

Still, we believe each of these personalities are just different sides of ourselves. And they *are*, in a sense that spatially speaking, they occupy the same space—our brain. And for us, everything that goes on inside our heads is just simply part of ourselves. Nothing more.

However, this way of thinking and experiencing things is a rather recent construction in human history, and even more, a largely western sensibility. This is the modern notion of the "buffered self," in contrast with the older and more widespread notion of the "porous self."[4] In our secular western society, we believe that we are essentially enclosed selves; that is, our minds, our inner thoughts and feelings are "buffered" and "closed off" from the outside. What is "inside" our mind is sharply distinguished from what is "outside" in the world. What is "outside" is not us; in contrast,

---

4. Taylor, *Secular Age*, 35–43.

we have complete ownership of whatever that is "inside," whether it's our thoughts or feelings or values or the personal meanings we imbue upon whatever we experience.

This view did take a blow at the beginning of the twentieth century when we discovered that much of what goes in our mind—much of our reasoning, desires, or motivations—is in fact, unconscious. We do not really "own" them, in that they are beyond our conscious control. But, we still believe those things are just us, even if an unconscious part.

So, that bright light that you see, perhaps from the fireworks from a local festival or a fiery meteor streaking overhead, is something that's "outside." But, if seeing that light makes you feel that you should move into that town to start a new life, that's something "inside" you. The light from the fireworks or meteor is not you, while the feeling that leads you to take up residence in that town is purely, and solely, you.

This way of thinking is contrasted with the notion of the self that is older, held by humanity for far longer, and even now is more widespread culturally—that of an open self. This self is "porous," so that what is "inside" you is open to what is "outside." The sudden inspiration you had in composing that music or a poem *is* you, but is *also* the goddess of inspiration. The vision of a shining figure telling you to save your country from foreign invaders is a vision you had, but is also a divine message that you received. The voices inside the arena of your mind that demand you to listen and follow are part of you, but they are also *more* than you, especially if what they have to say are particularly compelling or meaningful.

They are like "*emissaries*" of something beyond you.

"EMISSARIES" INSIDE US THAT SHAPE OUR LIVES

How we went from this open, "porous" self to the enclosed, "bounded" self—what influences and idiosyncrasies of western modernity led to the change—is described extensively by Charles Taylor's *Secular Age*, and we need not explore that here.

I'm simply pointing out that the idea of the self we tend to hold today, which assumes that all the voices that speak inside us are nothing more than just part of ourselves, is neither universal nor obvious. We may say that they are just processes in our brains. But, *everything* we experience, in that sense, is a process in the brain. This includes you reading this book, which is actually the firing of neurons in your eyes, transmitted to your brain, which then fires neurons that deal with language comprehension. Of course, what started that was from the "outside"—namely, this book—but the same can be said of whatever starts the debate between the voices. The line between "inside" and "outside" *blurs.*

And in an important way, these voices are indeed emissaries of something beyond you, because certain voices—and the personalities they represent—are not limited to *your* mind. Versions of them appear to other people too, across time, cultures, and societies, and they have moved people and shaped our history. In that sense, they are like *gods.*

They are certainly forces, and what you are experiencing is your personal version of those forces, playing out in your mind, presumably as your brain fires the relevant neural pathways. So, these voices may be speaking "inside," in your mind, but they also speak from beyond you, inside many other people's minds.[5]

An analogy here—and always be mindful of the limit of analogies—is a type of software, an app you download on a computer hardware, like your smartphone. This app runs locally on your phone and such, but there's something it's connected to, from which you and everyone else downloaded that app—from which it gets periodic updates even. Your computer is running that software, but the same software is running on others too, doing the *same thing*. This app is then both "inside" your computer, and "outside," beyond it.

But, does this really mean that these "voices" are some real entities out in the world? Aren't they still just some pervasive psychological feature of humanity? Christianity is actually ambivalent on this question. They may just be aspects of our collective unconscious, just things from our psyche. If so, we make them into idols when we follow them. Or, they may be active agents in reality, independent of us. If so, they'd be something like "gods." But "god" is not "God." They'd still be entities *in* our reality—what Christianity calls "powers" and "principalities," which are part of creation like us, part of the story of reality that the Creator is speaking forth.[6]

And Christianity is ambivalent on this question, because that is not what it's most concerned with. The real question for Christianity—and

---

5. This idea points to what the Swiss psychologist Carl Jung described as the archetypes that exist in humanity's "collective unconscious." For a detailed exploration of this idea, check Jung, *Archetypes and the Collective Unconscious.*

6. Eph 6:12; Col 1:16; 2:15.

What do you mean God "speaks to you"?

I would say, for most major religious and philosophical traditions of the world—is this: *Which voice should we listen to?*

You see, each voice, each personality—each emissary—represents a particular way we may relate to reality. Should we fight it, as a world of chaos and contests of strength? Should we regard it impassively, as a place to gather and hoard data? Should we revel in it, as a place to find and enjoy pleasure? Should we cringe from it, with fear and dread? Should we seethe with hatred and resentment toward it? Which way of relating to reality should we follow, and how far? And when, if ever, should we follow another way? Because each voice represents a way of living, and the way we live *embodies* what we believe Reality *is*.

And the question Christianity poses is, which voice, if followed, would enable us to relate to reality as a whole in such a way that we'll embody What—or Who—Reality truly is? Which voice speaks what is true, and not just true in one way, but true in *every* way? Which voice brings us to truthful, meaningful life, changing us for the good, bringing forth a better world, not only in some occasions, but in every occasion, *every* time we listen?

Because *that* is the voice of God speaking to us.

VOICE OF GOD SPEAKING INSIDE US

Here is where our analogies about God becomes crucial. Because in some analogies, a voice that speaks "inside" us can never be God. For example, in the analogy of God as an engineer who built a machine, we are "automatons," manufactured and activated as "buffered," "enclosed" systems. In such a picture, everything happening inside us is solely ourselves, and "God" can only speak *from the outside*—an entity trying to ping us, or worse, hack into our systems. Trapped in this analogy, we'll become preoccupied with the question of whether it's "all in our heads."

But, if *all* of *reality*—including our "innermost depths"—is God "speaking," and if all of history is like a story that God "authors," then God speaking *to* us means something different. A voice that speaks within us, or even our own thoughts, *can* be God speaking; after all, authors can pen the very thoughts of characters in their story. God can even speak to us an "outside" event that continues seamlessly to an "inside" thought, such as a child nearby singing, "take up and read," which propels us to read the Bible and follow what it says.[7]

---

7. This alludes to the pivotal event that led to Augustine's conversion, as recounted in *Confessions* 8.12.

"God"? What's That?

And if a voice that speaks inside our minds *is* God speaking to us, we can engage it in a conversation. Or rather, we can engage a voice that *may* be God. Because we usually won't know when we first engage.

But, when we do so, we may find that this voice seems to speak in ways that are not *quite* "us." All of us probably had experiences when a particularly powerful or surprising thought suddenly "came to us." Maybe it was an insight or realization, or a strong sense or feeling, or even actual words. It struck us, seemingly from nowhere. Which is an odd thing, really, if we have full ownership of everything that goes on in our mind. How does our own thought *surprise* us or "come to us"?

Of course, we can say that such thoughts must've emerged from our unconscious. But, if *all* of reality is God "speaking," it isn't very important *where* in that reality this thought came from. If anything, our unconscious seems a rather fitting way for the "Speaker" of all reality to personally speak something we'd never think ourselves. After all, our unconscious thoughts and feelings are beyond our conscious control. So, if God is to engage us in a genuine conversation, why not do so from our unconscious? The real question is not where this voice speaks from, but the *content* of what it says.

And it may have told you, as it did with Abraham, to move from your place of safety and comfort and step into the unknown; that you must do so, because the life that will bring you greater meaning and transform your world for the better cannot be had where you are. And it is then that you must ask: Is this really the voice of God? Which is to say, is what this voice is speaking *true*?

And sometimes you immediately *know* that it's true, because deep in your heart, you've known what the truth was. For example, you've been filled with resentment against your brother, which you know is unfair and petty. The voice speaks up and asks whether you're truly in the right to be resentful. You make excuses to justify yourself, but that voice inside you calmly replies, "You know that none of that's true." You were the one who was unfair to him and you need to change your ways. It says that if you keep on this course, you'll become a warped, distorted version of yourself. Perhaps, you will listen. Or perhaps, you'll ignore the voice, and ignore it every time it speaks up, until it speaks up no more—until the thought that corrects you no longer "comes" to you. That's the biblical story of Cain and Abel; it's what happened to Cain before he murdered his brother.[8]

---

8. Gen 4:3–9.

But sometimes this voice may reveal truth that you cannot know. That voice may have spoken as you were gazing at the strange sight of a bush that's on fire yet somehow does not burn. The sight was reminding you of your people, enslaved in a distant land and suffering as if set on fire, but refusing to simply burn away. Again, it may be that the burning bush is actually a physical phenomenon in the "outside" world, while the voice is speaking "inside" you—or vice versa—but that distinction is irrelevant here. What is relevant is that the voice is speaking. And it calls to you and declares that your people will be freed. It directs you to go to the most powerful ruler of your world, the one who holds your people in slavery, and tell him to free your people.

But you respond, "There's no way anyone, let alone a ruler, will listen to me." Yet, that voice is persistent. It replies that reality will unfold whatever needs to happen, *to happen*, to free your people.

This voice spoke to you, you replied, and it answered. Whether this is a mental conversation, or a physically audible one, is not important. What *is* important is whether the voice is speaking the *truth*.

And in this particular story, the voice itself sets out the criteria to answer this question. When your people are freed from slavery and return here with you, you'll know that this voice indeed was *God speaking*. Which is probably not too comforting an answer for you. But, start out you must. Because you cannot know if this voice is God unless you embark on the journey to see for yourself whether it spoke the truth.

And *that's* the story of Moses and the exodus from Egypt.[9]

Now, what makes this the voice of God, rather than simply some unconscious part of Moses that hoped for the liberation of his people, is that this voice was leading him to attempt something *he* deemed impossible—things far beyond what he can imagine. And if he failed, it'd mean that the voice was not speaking the truth.

And it is here that we can begin to understand the idea of miracles in the Bible.

MIRACLES ARE FIRSTLY ABOUT COMMUNICATION

We who live in a Godless world tend to think that miracles are something that "violates" the laws of Nature; Hawking, for example, called them "exceptions to the laws." This again is rooted in the defunct analogy that

9. Exod 3:1—4:20.

"God"? What's That?

God created our universe like how an engineer would manufacture a machine. Once the machine is complete and turned on, *anything* God does is something that "interferes" with how this machine runs. And *that* is what miracles are supposed to be in this analogy. And none of that has anything to do with what Christianity actually means by miracles. Or God.

In the Bible, the word "miracle" has a two-fold meaning.[10] First is that it is something that brings us to marvel and wonder; this, of course, includes things *we* deem to be impossible. But this isn't about interfering with the operations of a machine-like universe. After all, our entire speech-like reality—including all its principles and laws—is God speaking. And "miracle" is part of that *everything* God speaks; but there is something special to what God speaks that brings us to marvel.

Did you notice that "us" is part of the meaning? Miracles are about *communication*. God is speaking forth something that will bring *us* to marvel. So, the second meaning of miracle is that it is a "sign." What is it a sign of? That the voice you're following is speaking the truth; the voice that spoke to you *is* God, and not merely your own thoughts and imagination. Miracles unfold *from* our conversation with God.

Here's an interesting case-study. A study at the National Center for Atmospheric Research in the U.S., which was published in the journal PLoS ONE in 2010, simulated the parting of the sea, as described in the book of Exodus. The study wasn't trying to prove the Bible; it was just applying fluid dynamics to an interesting case study. And it found that a natural phenomenon known as a "wind setdown"—specifically, a gale force east wind as described in the biblical story—would cause the water of a large lake in the Eastern Nile Delta to part into walls few meters high, making a land path people could cross.[11] At least, it would according to the simulations that followed the laws of physics. Now, the question is, is this a miracle?

If we think a miracle is God violating some law of Nature, then it's *not*. But, in the proper biblical definition, the parting of the sea is really about

---

10. Padgett, "God and Miracle in an Age of Science," 533. Padgett also introduces an insightful set of definitions for "miracle" in the context of scientific understanding of Nature and its laws. He first points out how contemporary science has found "physical laws" to be probabilistic rather than deterministic, so that most of the events that seem to go against these laws are "strictly extraordinary events," rather than an impossibility. Miracles can also be "physically impossible" events too. But, whether a physical impossibility or just an extraordinary event, something is a miracle if it points us to God. See Padgett, "God and Miracle in an Age of Science," 534–37.

11. Drews and Han, "Dynamics of Wind Setdown."

what God has been speaking to Moses and the Israelites. In the story, they were trapped between the sea and the Egyptian army chasing them, so they cried out to God. After all, if the Egyptians caught them and killed them all, it'd mean that the voice that had been speaking to Moses had not spoken the truth; it would not have been the voice of God. But God speaks again, and a wind blows upon the waters, parting the sea and opening a path for the Israelites to escape. It was a sign that this voice spoke the truth to Moses.

Compare that with another scenario. Let's say you were out for a walk by the seashore, and the sea parted. There's no natural explanation for it. But let's say it also *meant nothing to you*; it left no mark in your life other than as once-in-a-lifetime selfie. To call *that* a miracle seems to be missing something. Because for Christianity, miracles are part of the conversation between us and God. They reveal *Who* is speaking.

But, God speaking to us does not always require miracles. Because again, the primary character of hearing God speak is *truth*. And not every truth we need to hear requires a miracle for us to know it's true.

CHAPTER SEVEN

What do you mean the Bible is "God's Word"?

If you've been to a church service, you may have seen someone stand up to read from the Bible and then close by saying, "This is the word of the Lord"—that is, "the word of Yahweh." This is because Christians believe that the Bible is the "Word of God"; it's something that God speaks. When they say, "God's word," that's what they're usually referring to.

Except that according to Christianity, *all* of *reality* is God speaking. And God can speak to us from *any*where in that reality, and especially as a voice that speaks from within us. So then, why is the Bible specifically identified as the "Word of God?" What's so special about a book that was written thousands of years ago, about people who lived back then?

And the short answer is: the Bible is like a *map*. It's there to keep us from becoming lost when we try to hear God speaking in *everything*.

"GOD SPEAKING" MEANS MORE THAN JUST THE BIBLE

So, what does it mean to say that the Bible is the "Word of God"?

This question, by the way, is at the very foundation of the more popular disputes today about whether the Bible has errors. These are questions about whether there are inconsistencies or inaccuracies in the Bible, or if science conflicts with its account of how our universe came into being. Such questions arose because, again, to hear God speak is to hear *truth*; that is its fundamental character. So, if the Bible is "God's word," whatever

What do you mean the Bible is "God's Word"?

it says must be true.[1] And presumably, that means it cannot have errors in any of these things.

However, what an error is depends on *what kind* of truth is being communicated. Here's an example. When Neil Armstrong stepped off the Moon Lander and planted his feet on the lunar surface on July 20, 1969, he said, "That's one small step for a man, one giant leap for mankind." Now, was that statement an error? Since collectively speaking, human beings as a species—"mankind"—have leapt higher, longer, and from greater distances. Armstrong's step was no leap—it was more like a tiny hop, really. But, it's obvious to us that that was *not* what he was saying; that wasn't the truth he was communicating.

So, what kind of truth is the Bible communicating? This is the question of biblical interpretation. We need to understand *what* the Bible is communicating before we can ask, is *that* true?

And this returns us to the question of what it really means to say that the Bible is the "Word of God." Because it turns out that what Christianity means by that is something very specific, even if it's not always clearly articulated. After all, the phrase, "God speaking," refers to much, much more than just the Bible.

In fact, we've seen how quite literally *everything* is God "speaking." Our entire speech-like reality—among infinite others that also could've been—is God "speaking." The entire story-like history of the universe, life, and humanity is God "speaking." That's what it means to say that God is the Creator and Sustainer of all things. This in turn means that *every* truth that we can ever come to know, whether through insight, inspiration, introspection, inquiry, or investigation, is us becoming in*formed* by what God is speaking.

And God also speaks *to us*. According to Christianity, we *can*, with effort, come to know that our reality is something *like* speech, spoken by a "Speaker"—that is to say, we can know that all things were created by

---

1. Strictly speaking, even in this view, not everything written *in* the Bible is "true," since there are times when people or entities in the Bible—such as the devil—lie; in such cases, what the Bible reports *about* what they said is true. This seems to be splitting hairs, but that's how it is. This version of "biblical inerrancy" we have today, which insists that the Bible can have no error in the literal sense regarding factual matters, seems to be a relatively recent position, from post-Reformation polemics. See Hendel, "Dream of a Perfect Text," 524–31. But, both "inerrancy" and its competing position of "infallibility"—that the Bible will not lead us astray regarding our relation to God—derive from the common Christian teaching that the Bible was written by the inspiration of God's Spirit, and thus something that God has spoken to us.

God. But we cannot know *Who* the Speaker is unless the Speaker speaks *to us*. This is the idea of "revelation," which presents us with a more specific meaning of what Christians mean by the "Word of God." The Bible is such *revelation* from God—God speaking to us.[2]

However, God can speak to us in many, many other ways, since all of reality is God speaking. God can speak to us through creation. God can speak to us through what happens around us—so, God who spoke to Moses then spoke and unfolded the events that freed the Israelites from their enslavement in Egypt. God can also speak to us as the voice of truth, speaking in prophetic messages, visions, promptings in our innermost self, or some profound personal experiences. Every such personal encounter with God can constitute "revelation."[3]

So, where does the Bible *fit* in all of that? Why do Christians insist on bestowing their Bible with the title, "the Word of God," if *everything* is God speaking and everything *can* be God speaking *to* us? And we who live in this Godless world tend to misunderstand the answer.

We tend to get it backwards.

WE NEED THE BIBLE *BECAUSE* EVERYTHING IS GOD SPEAKING

Those of us who argue about whether the Bible is "God's word" often seem to get into this dichotomy where knowing God through the Bible is pitted against knowing God—or Reality—through *other* means. So, there's Bible on the one side and things like personal experiences, meditation, communing with Nature, or even philosophical or scientific inquiry on the other. On the one end of the spectrum are certain kind of Christians who seem to reject everything in the latter list, leaving the Bible as the only way of knowing what God is speaking. On the other end are people who reject that the Bible is the Word of God—that this old book holds no truth about our reality. Then, there are those in the middle, saying that we can know God through both.

---

2. Aquinas presents Christian theology as knowledge drawn from such revelation, which he then identifies as "Scriptures." See Aquinas, *ST* I.q1.aa1–3. See also Calvin, *Institutes*, 1.6.

3. For a concise overview of this idea of revelation in Christian theology, and different models of what revelation consists of, see McGrath, *Christian Theology*, 135–45.

What do you mean the Bible is "God's Word"?

However, I think that this entire spectrum misses why Christianity actually needs the Bible. We need the Bible not simply to know what God is speaking to us, but to know what God is *not* speaking.

Perhaps that was bit too provocative a way of putting it. What I'm pointing out is that if we carefully consider what Christianity means by God "speaking," the long list that we've summed up just before, we'd realize that this raises a very significant, practical problem. Because literally *everything* is God speaking—and that's a *huge* problem.

After all, *which* is it? Which out of this everything is something that God is speaking *to us*? Which out of everything we experience, and every thought that comes to us, is meaningful and true, and which of *those* are untainted from distortion or self-deception, so that it *is* God speaking to us? And how do we know?

Here's an example. Let's say your recent hospital visit has left you short on money to pay the rent next week—because you live in the U.S., not Canada. Having run out of options, you pray to God. Then, you notice a wallet, fallen on the sidewalk. When you pick it up, you find that this wallet belongs to your landlord, but it also has enough cash to pay the rent. Now, the fallen wallet *is* God speaking; your finding that wallet is God speaking; that it belongs to your landlord is also God speaking. But, just *what* is God speaking *to you* through all this?

So, different thoughts come to you as you hold the wallet. One says that God has given you this wallet to pay your rent; another reminds you that your landlord has always been quite rude to you, and you're entitled to a bit of payback. But there's another that says you should return the wallet regardless. Which of these is God speaking to you? And why? If everything is God speaking, we need a guide that enable us to discern what God is speaking *to us* from *all of that*.

Here's another example. Let's say that there's a very successful company owned by a Christian who is very active in the local church. And his company hired undocumented migrants off the record because they'll work well below minimum wage under substandard conditions. One day, one of the workers collapses due to overwork and poor health, and the whole deal gets exposed. But, the owner uses his influence in the community to avoid legal repercussions while the migrant workers are deported. And he starts telling others, "God protects those who believe in him." Is that what God is speaking to him? Is his success, which after all *is* part of everything God is speaking and unfolding, saying that God approves what he's been doing?

"GOD"? WHAT'S THAT?

Everything is God unfolding something. But the question is, what is God personally saying to us through it at any given time? And perhaps more importantly, what is God *not* saying?

Twenty-eight hundred years ago, the kingdom of Israel, whose citizens called themselves the people of God, was at the height of its power. Under its king, Jeroboam II, Israel's mighty armies subjugated their neighbors, the royal coffers were filled to the brim with wealth, and Jeroboam's palaces were marvels of artistic and architectural skill. Surely Israel's successes were God saying that they were favored! After all, they were fastidious with their religious rituals and had given God many, many offerings. Then a prophet named Amos spoke up.

And his message to Israel, recorded in the book of Amos in the Bible, was this: God indeed unfolds all things, and what God will now unfold for you is judgment. For you piled your wealth by exploiting the poor and wielded power to oppress the vulnerable. Your worship of God is tainted with your moral failures, and your true allegiance is with the idols that let you do this. Though you've grown rich and powerful, you do *not* have God's approval nor favor. And God will bring you down one day, along with your injustices and your false worship.[4]

However, the book also reports that the head priest of Israel at that time denounced Amos as a troublemaker and a liar, then drove him out of the country. So, what *was* God speaking to Israel in all this? Blessing? Or warning? Jeroboam's dynasty fell after a few generations, and the kingdom of Israel was eventually destroyed and sent to exile. So, the Bible sides with Amos as the one who spoke the truth. As to *why* God sometimes unfolds success for an unjust nation in the first place, that's another question—though we'll touch on that in a later chapter.

The Christian idea of the Bible is *not* that it's simply the record of what God spoke, let alone the only means of God speaking to us. Rather, the Bible is like a *map* that God draws for us regarding what He is speaking. At least, that's how we're translating the idea.

A map, by the way, doesn't show everything. In fact, a map is very selective in what it represents; it may show topography, or state boundaries, or roads and cities, but not everything. What a map shows depends on its *purpose*, which is to guide us through the place depicted on the map. And without the map, we can become lost as we journey across the world that is drawn on it.

---

4. For the actual prophecies, read Amos 2:6—9:15.

WHAT DO YOU MEAN THE BIBLE IS "GOD'S WORD"?

All of reality is God speaking, and every truth is us hearing God speak. But the Bible is the map that guides us, so that we do not get lost in the *infinity* of God's Speech, which composes literally everything there is. It charts a way to discern *when* God is speaking *personally to us* and marks the bounds of what God would *not* say. This in turn sketches just how we are to encounter, establish, and maintain a personal, ongoing relationship with God who speaks with us. That's why even in this book, every chapter that "translates" the Christian idea of God also references the Bible; it's checking where our translations point to in the map.

What is remarkable, though, is *how* the Bible draws this map.

THE BIBLE DRAWS THE MAP BY A MOSAIC OF LIFE-STORIES

As holy books go, the Christian Bible is a rather strange book. It's a hodgepodge of stories, chronicles, biographies, reflections, poems, prayers, prophecies, dialogues, letters, and treatises. And it is composed by numerous authors from wildly different backgrounds, over a span of some thousand years or so. These authors wrote what God spoke to them, in the many, many different ways that God personally speaks to people. And nearly all of its content—except for the account of God creating the world—is about the lives of people: particular individuals, communities, or nations, how they lived, what they thought, and what they did.

Much of it is simply the *stories* of such people, rather than records of some teachings or a discourse.[5] And instead of limiting these stories to that of a single or even a handful of exemplary individuals, the Bible runs a gamut of heroes and villains, successes, failures, and mediocrities, and at times, the same person can become all of those at one time or another. And a surprisingly large number of these stories do not provide a clear lesson or a message, leaving the readers puzzled over what the moral or spiritual teaching was, or whether there even was one. Then, there are the poems or

---

5. This core characteristic of the Bible has led to the idea of "narrative theology" in Christianity today, which points to narratives and stories as the primary way of describing God and humanity. According to this idea, narratives are not merely illustrations or examples, but the very fabric of revelation, through which God is experienced. A contemporary work that has recovered this idea for Christian theology today is *The Eclipse of Biblical Narrative* by Hans Frei. For a concise overview of this position, see McGrath, *Christian Theology*, 113–15.

prayers these people say that seem to be just pure lament, or even outright complaints or protests toward God.

Even when the reader is presented with more definitive teachings, from say, the prophets, or in the case of the New Testament, the sermons of Jesus or the letters of the apostles, the Bible specifies the particular context in which they were given. *When* the prophecy was spoken, or the sermon was preached, or the letter was written, and by *whom* and *to* whom. What was going on at the time, and what people were concerned with then. Of course, scholars can discern such contexts in the texts and teachings of other religions and philosophies. But the Bible seems to go out of its way each time to explicitly provide these contexts—if not right then and there, then elsewhere.

It's as if the Bible is trying to emphasize that real people, people like you and me, though living in a different time and place, went through these things. And they reacted like real people, sometimes inspiringly, sometimes with wisdom, but sometimes with pettiness, spitefulness, and deceit. And *this* is how they heard God, struggled over what they heard, wondered whether it was true, and talked or even argued among themselves. They then followed, or rejected, or distorted the truth that was spoken to them. And then, what was spoken to them came true. Perhaps they were promised miracles—extraordinary events that would confirm what they heard—which then unfolded in their lives. Or perhaps their lives unraveled because they rejected or distorted what they heard. Then, the next generation continued from where the previous generation left off.

So, the Bible follows these life-stories across generations, which flows together into a millennia-spanning story of a people. Long ago, they encountered something that spoke to them. And they followed what this voice spoke, and tried to live it out. They sang and prayed; they protested and rebelled. They wrestled with how to live in a right relation to reality, to other people, and to themselves. They cheated and betrayed and lost. They changed their ways, renewed their vows, relearned what they lost, and expanded on what they learned.

Through that long history, they continued to develop and refine their understanding of this "god" that their ancestors encountered. They used imagery and imagination to grasp what they could not understand, drawing upon metaphors and analogies where simple descriptions failed. And they learned that this "god" who spoke to them was *God*—Reality, speaking and unfolding all things, from the mundane to the miraculous.

The Bible is a "map," meant to guide us through that ongoing relationship with the God that speaks to us. But that map is composed of a vast *mosaic* of the life-stories of people and their journeys with God, generation after generation.

And this, in turn, raises two crucial ideas in Christianity regarding what it means to hear God personally speaking to us.

GOD SPEAKING TO US IS "ACCOMMODATED" TO WHERE WE ARE

Those of us who try to read the Bible today tend to run headfirst into this one, particular barrier. The Bible sometimes say things that seem *clearly* wrong today, scientifically or morally. Its creation account seems to conflict with what modern science says regarding our universe. It also seems to overlook or even support things that we'd regard as outright wrong morally, such as the harsh way people conduct wars or mete out justice, or in maintaining terrible inequalities in its society, such as slavery. And many of us will criticize the Bible for this.

But, scholars would argue that this is a misguided response. Science as we know it did not even exist until about three hundred years ago or so. And the book of Genesis is an ancient Hebrew text, and much of its view of the world was the same as that of other Middle-Eastern civilizations of their time. Likewise, when the Old Testament accounts of wars, violence, and inequalities shock modern readers, they caution that we should not unthinkingly apply our modern ethical sensibility to the Iron Age culture of the people in the Bible. And in both cases, they are correct. But, not correct *enough*.

Because our question is: If the Bible is *God* speaking to people, why did God not speak *correct* things to them? For example, why did God not teach modern scientific knowledge or ethical standards to those who wrote the Hebrew Bible—the Christian Old Testament?

However, leaving aside our rather overconfident assumption that the final, ultimate truth about the universe or morality will be anywhere close to our modern views, we should ask, if *that* kind of truth is what the Bible was trying to teach. Suppose that such scientific or ethical truths were spoken to the people in the Bible; would they have been able to even comprehend them, let alone *live* by them? We are talking about a people that—according to Jesus a thousand years later—God had to set out a legal procedure for dismissing their wives with a divorce, because they were having a hard time accepting that they weren't allowed to just throw them out whenever they wanted.[6] The Bible is written for real people, living in a real society, with real limitations and failings.

So, demanding that the biblical texts—which were written by and for the ancient Hebrews and then first-century Christians—somehow present modern scientific truths or ethical norms is rather like demanding that the explorers who sailed around the world for the first time in history should have done so on a nuclear-powered submarine. The people we'd be asking for are *not real*. And of course, we'd be completely missing the point of learning about those first explorers.

This is why the Bible *needs* to be a text of ancient Hebrews, or first-century Christians, with their limited knowledge about the world, the cosmos, and beyond, and holding some ethical standard that we may now find archaic. It *needs* to be a text from such people, who lived among the Middle-Eastern and Mediterranean civilizations. Because that's what makes them a *real people* who lived in *real times*. And only real people, with real limitations, and real mistakes, can have a real relation to Reality—a real personal relationship with God.

Of course, we can't really explore this issue without going into actual examples. Could God have spoken a "more scientifically accurate" version of the creation account to the ancient Hebrews who recorded the book of Genesis? If not, *why not*? And the answer would depend on what kind of truth the Genesis account was trying to communicate to the people back then and, in turn, to *us*. But we'll have to explore such questions in another book since we're still translating basic ideas.

However, here's a general *caveat* regarding what it means for God to speak to us, according to Christianity. In chapter 4, we explored how all our words about God—including every human-like trait—are analogies; they are the best *we* can do to characterize the infinite Reality with the language and concepts available to us. The following caveat is the other side of that very same principle; just as what *we* say of God is constrained by our limits, what God speaks *to us* is constrained for the same reason. Everything God speaks to us is thus "accommodated" to our current limit of understanding and cultural standards.[7]

---

6. Matt 5:31–32; Mark 10:1–12.

7. McGrath, *Christian Theology*, 169–70. "Accommodation" is a key idea in Christian theology regarding the Bible. Calvin, for example, wrote that God speaks with us

What do you mean the Bible is "God's Word"?

To understand this idea, imagine a father working one evening, coding a complex set of instructions for an A.I. of a video game. Then, his child comes into his study and climbs up on his lap. She then peers into the screen and then asks what he's doing. Now, the father can talk about the latest machine-learning algorithms, or coding languages, or how these codes are processed at the level of hardware. But she won't understand any of that. So, he says instead that he's "teaching" the computer how to play a game. That's the answer that his child can understand and, more to the point, that's what she was really asking him. So, he's "accommodating" his answer to his child.

And when the Bible was being written, God was not accommodating to us living in our modern age. It was to ancient Israelites, the Jews during and after the Babylonian exile, and to the first-century Christians; it was to *their* worldview, their culture, and their level of understanding that God was "accommodating" what was being spoken.

This is *not* at all to say that the Bible simply affirms everything the people back then believed; it posed significant challenges to their entire world in all its aspects; but, it did so at a level they could still understand, so that they could change themselves. Because that's how we relate to reality as we reach new truths or try to build a better world. We start from *where we currently are*; our journeys are taken in steps, not flights. And each such step is an engagement *with* God.

We who live in a Godless world have tended to imagine God as some powerful alien entity in our reality. So, we tend to think that the recorded "word" of this entity should be some kind of artifact that uplifts our civilization to some utopian age in a single bound. But, God is *Reality*—reality with which we're engaged even now. And the Bible is a map that guides us in how we relate to this reality, hearing God speak *each* and *every step* of our life-journey. And it does not present us with warp-gates or wormholes that will let us skip this journey.

However, it does present us with a *person* who'll walk alongside us through it all. For that is what this map is meant to reveal: a person.

---

in the Bible as with children to "accommodate" to the "feebleness" of our knowledge. See Calvin, *Institutes*, 1.13.1. More than a thousand years before him, Augustine wrote how Scripture "descend" to our "capacity" and matches our gaits "like a mother." See Augustine, *Literal Meaning of Genesis*, 2.6.13; 5.3.6; 5.6.19.

THE MAP THAT THE BIBLE DRAWS IS A PORTRAIT OF A PERSON

The Bible is a millennia-spanning mosaic of life-stories of a people who wrestled with the God that spoke to them. In a sense, it is a collection of case-studies, and each case presents how a voice spoke to a people and how they responded, and what reality then unfolded. It is from these that each generation spoke their prayers, sang their psalms, and set forth their teachings and laws.

And with each case, each generation, one after another, the portrait of Reality came into clearer focus. And it pointed to *which* voice, among the many voices, was the one that spoke to them the truth and unfolded reality. Because the vast set of life-stories across generations revealed that this voice—the voice that spoke true—revealed a consistent kind of *character*, a *personality*. Very different people heard this voice "speak," in very different ways—an inner voice, or a sudden thought, or a vivid dream or a vision, or some fiery conviction. And they heard this voice in different historical circumstances, in different kinds of society, with different cultural norms and worldviews. Even the wording and style of what was spoken differed depending on who heard this voice. But, the *character* of this voice remained constant.

That was the voice of God—the voice of Reality. This was what those who mapped out the great journey of the Bible encountered and experienced. The voice that spoke the truth, the voice that guided them and unfailingly unfolded reality, from the mundane to the miraculous, every time and in every circumstance, revealed the *same kind of person*. And *that* is what Christianity ultimately means by the "Word of God."

The "Word of God" is the Logos, our entire speech-like reality; the "Word of God" is the life-stories of people who spoke and journeyed with the "Speaker" of that reality; the "Word of God" is also the written record of these stories, the Bible. But this "Word of God" in turn painted a portrait of this "Speaker" as a particular kind of person.[8]

And what every Christian believes and confesses is that this person was fully revealed in one historical individual: Jesus Christ. It was "Jesus" who fully embodied the character of the voice of God in a way no other

---

8. McGrath, *Christian Theology*, 112–13.

human being could. That is what the Gospel of John means when it declares in its opening that the Logos became a human being and dwelt among us.[9]

And this confession presents a very significant idea for our time. The most important kind of truth, truth that will endure in a world where nothing seems true, is a kind of *person*.

---

9. John 1:14a.

CHAPTER EIGHT

There's truth, then there's truth that generates truths

"What is truth?"

That was what Pontius Pilate asked before he ordered Jesus to be flogged and then crucified.

That is how this Roman governor over the province of Judea ended his interrogation of that Jewish man, charged with sedition by religious leaders of the day. He had asked him: "Are you the king of the Jews?" Are you claiming to be a king, inciting a rebellion against our empire? And that man had answered, "My kingdom is not of this world. If it were, my servants would fight to prevent my arrest. The reason I was born and came into the world is to testify to the truth. Everyone on the side of truth listens to me."[1]

That was when Pilate retorted, "What is truth?" He left without waiting for a reply, to meet the man's accusers waiting outside. Then, he said to them, "I find no basis for a charge against him." But those who wanted that man dead were powerful, prominent members of society. So, to appease them, the governor had the man flogged and then executed by crucifixion. After all, *what is truth*?

This question is not about some philosophical definition. It's about what really is true in a world where "truth" is so often bought by power and sold to the highest bidder. If truth is about our intellect's adequacy to reality, is there any belief, or theory, or idea that can stand the test of that definition? Is there really any truth to the things we believe and commit to, when our "truth" is constantly being corroded?

---

1. This conversation between Pilate and Jesus takes place in John 18:28–40.

And the Christian Gospels have presented the following answer: Truth we are to seek and find, first and foremost, is a kind of *person*. For it is that truth that *generates* other truths. And every truth that this generates for us is "hearing God speaking."

OUR POST-TRUTH WORLD IS AN ASSAULT TO THE "PERSONALITY" OF TRUTH

It seems we now live in a "post-truth" world; the term was the Oxford word of the year in 2016, describing a condition in which facts matter less than personal beliefs in shaping public opinion.[2] In short, we'll believe whatever we want, and whether it's *true* no longer matters.

But, is that what's really going on? Does our post-truth world reject the very notion of truth? Is that why we're becoming increasingly polarized in our views, as we cocoon ourselves in echo chambers, consuming disinformation and lies? Because there's no such thing as truth anyway? Because we think there simply is *no reality* beyond what we want to believe?[3] Then, our efforts so far to translate "God" would be for naught; those translations would find no footing in such a world.

However, I don't think that's the case. For one thing, even some Christians—specifically, creationists—are described as having this "post-truth" mindset.[4] And if anything, the more extreme our views and more polarized our society, the more insistent we seem to be regarding the truth of our beliefs. And I don't mean we act with greater conviction; I mean we become less willing to *hear* anything else; we stop speaking with anyone who thinks differently. Scream, sneer, and slander, yes—but speak, not so much. In fact, we could probably find easy examples of such people from those who hold

---

2. *Oxford Languages*, "Word of the Year 2016." For a concise philosophical examination of the issue, see McIntyre, *Post-Truth*. But the conceptual framework to understand "post-truth," as a political and social phenomenon, was already being theorized by thinkers like Hannah Arendt, who penned these following words: "The ideal subject of totalitarian rule is not the convinced Nazi or the convinced Communist, but people for whom the distinction between fact and fiction (i.e., the reality of experience) and the distinction between true and false (i.e., the standards of thought) no longer exist" (*Origins of Totalitarianism*, 474).

3. McIntyre phrases this question this way: "What seems new in the post-truth era is a challenge not just to the idea of knowing reality, but to the existence of reality itself" (*Post-Truth*, 10).

4. McIntyre, *Post-Truth*, 143. Creationists would in turn accuse their detractors of the same thing.

views we oppose—regarding politics, morality, or religion; though oddly enough, we tend to have a much harder time finding such people on "our side."

And our post-truth world takes this to its extreme; what we believe *must* be true, so whatever that goes against it *must* be wrong somehow. Consequently, we'll ignore any facts or findings that counter our views, and censure anyone who points to them, whether they be scientists, journalists, or even family. But we'll magnify any findings that support our views, and idolize anyone who affirms them, whether they be politicians, YouTube hosts, or conspiracy theorists. So, "truth" seems as important as ever in our post-truth world; it's just that we regard truth as something we already possess, and only the facts that confirm it matter.[5]

Such a mindset is closer to totalitarianism, rather than some nihilistic stance toward truth. If we think our truth is simply unquestionable, we cannot help but see those who oppose it as either incomprehensibly ignorant or evil. And we cannot speak with such people; we must instead impose our truth upon them while *our* side has the power; we must run them off our campuses, shut down their media, and appoint our people to the court. That's probably why elections in our democracies feel more and more like death matches. Because it's no longer about electing a leader; it's about raising a champion to put down the other side.

And in such a world, truth is no longer something that guides our steps, exhorting us to seek and find. "Truth" instead becomes something that *possesses* us, compelling us to hunt and *feed*. For such truth sustains itself only by the silence of dissent. And so, at its terminal stage, we who live in a post-truth world will indeed *thirst* for "truth," but not like pilgrims for water, but like vampires for blood.

But, what drives us to this? A Canadian psychologist, Jordan Peterson, remarked that "nihilism [is the] alter-ego of totalitarianism."[6] Truths that we fight over, truths we seek to impose upon others, aren't mere factual truths. These are the larger truths about the very world in which we live and the paths we are to take in it, and facts are but bricks we use to build these kinds of truths. And if we lose *these* truths—if we fall into the nihilism that such a

---

5. McIntyre describes this as "a corruption of the process by which facts are credibly gathered and reliably used to shape one's beliefs about reality" (*Post-Truth*, 11); see also 35–62.

6. Peterson, *Maps of Meaning*, 265. It is thus both ironic and fitting that Peterson himself has become a central figure in the kind of polemic that follows the very dynamic he has described.

loss would bring—we'll find ourselves lost in a world that these truths kept away. Everything we fear in life awaits us there: our family evicted from our homes; a society that controls our speech and actions; a world ravaged by droughts, wildfires, and floods. A divided, post-truth society does not reject truth; each side fears the loss of its larger truths, and pivots toward totalitarianism. Because we'll do anything to preserve the truths we believe will keep our worst fears from happening.[7]

But, my purpose here isn't to raise alarms about what's currently happening in our society. There are plenty of others doing that.

What I'm trying to point out is that even in the extreme case of a post-truth world, the fundamental question that confronts us is still about our *relation* to reality.[8] It is, in Christian terms, about "hearing" God "speaking."

But in a post-truth world, this relation has been twisted backward. It is not us who must conform *our* logos to that of reality; instead, we act as if reality is to conform *its* Logos to ours. That is, God is to "speak" what we demand to "hear." Of course, that's not what we actually think we're doing. We think reality is already the way we say it is, so there's nothing more we need to hear.

And in doing this, we're not rejecting the notion of truth *or* of reality; we're rejecting *how* we are to engage reality. To put it differently, we're trying to bury our trodden path to truth.

THE PATH TO TRUTH, FROM METHODS TO PERSON

How *do* we come to know the truth? This remains a perennial question of philosophy. We've been asking what are the means, the methods, the paths, to reliably *reach* the *truth*.

Nowadays, we tend to think of science when we're asked this question—if we believe we *can* know any truth, that is. But science is essentially

---

7. I will let Peterson's opening to his book speak here: "Something we cannot see protects us from something we do not understand. The thing we cannot see is culture, in its intrapsychic or internal manifestation. The thing we do not understand is the chaos that gave rise to culture. If the structure of culture is disrupted, unwittingly, chaos returns. We will do anything—anything—to defend ourselves against that return" (*Maps of Meaning*, xi).

8. This is how McIntyre concludes his book, remarking that "post-truth is not about reality; it's about the way that humans react to reality" (*Post-Truth*, 172). To put it more specifically, we aren't really doing away with truth, we're simply pretending that reality is siding with us.

a highly refined form of a more general and fundamental process through which we come to know things.[9] This was the insight of Bernard Lonergan, a Catholic philosopher, who identified this process in terms of four cognitive operations through which we engage reality. First is experience, which includes sense data and introspection. Second is understanding, which interprets our experience and forms insights or hypotheses. Third is judgment, which evaluates this understanding through critical reason and further experience. Then fourth is decision, which is about practical and ethical implications of our new knowledge.

In science, these four correspond to gathering data, forming a hypothesis, testing the hypothesis, and then considering the ethical question raised by our findings. For an example of the ethical question: If we find that humans are causing climate change, what ought we to do about it?

But we also navigate our everyday life with these operations. Say, you're a manager of a company and your department is performing poorly. You then—if you're a good manager—investigate; you check the numbers on work hours and productivity, and conduct interviews. You then come up with some ideas of what's happening. Maybe you have employees who are unqualified, inadequately trained, or have bad work habits. You then test your idea by going over their work. But it turns out that they know what they're doing and work very hard. Then, your investigation finds something else. They tend to perform poorly right after you give them their tasks; some employees complained in their interviews that your instructions aren't clear; when you had a veteran employee give out the instructions instead, performance rose. Now, you have an ethical quandary. Do you acknowledge your fault in this and change your ways, or hide the results to spare your pride?

These operations, in turn, present us with what Lonergan called the "transcendental precepts."[10] Be attentive—pay attention to everything you experience. Be intelligent—seek understanding of what's going on. Be reasonable—make judgements by critically evaluating your ideas. And be responsible—act with integrity regarding what you learn. Yet, these are not some methods or algorithms; they are exhortations to be a certain *kind of person*. And this is emphasized when Lonergan adds a fifth precept: "Be in love," which is the *motivation* for seeking truth.

---

9. Lonergan, *Method in Theology*, 4.
10. Lonergan, *Method in Theology*, 231, 268.

So, the path to truth is a *person*; that is what these precepts point to. That is the central Christian claim. Truth is a *person*, pointing first and finally to the one who declared, "I am the way, the truth, and the life."[11]

To really understand the importance of this idea though, we need to turn to another challenge to the notion of truth today: postmodernism.

WE CAN NEVER SEPARATE "US" FROM OUR TRUTHS

Now, I've heard some popular depictions of postmodernism as a denial of objective truth and even of reality independent of our beliefs. If you ever heard people say things like, "well, your reality is not my reality," or "every truth is relative anyway," this is where it comes from. And if that's what postmodernism is arguing, it would truly be a "post-truth" position.[12] But, while these depictions do have *some* basis, they tend to blur a key distinction—a distinction crucial for our translations of "God."

Generally speaking, postmodernism does *not* deny that there really *is* reality independent of our beliefs. Otherwise, it'd be arguing that we could just believe that there's no such thing as gravity, and float into the sky. What postmodernism denies is that there is only one, true, objective *description of* reality. To put it in terms of our translations, postmodernists would not deny "Reality," nor, generally, even that our reality is speech-like—they'd not deny "God" nor "God speaking." What they would deny is that there's one, true, objective way *we* can speak what "*God*" is "speaking." But what does that really mean?

I'd summarize their position as the following: every truth *we* hold is necessarily *our* truth.[13] This seemingly obvious point has profound implications though. Our descriptions of reality—truths we hold—are constrained and shaped by who we are and where we are: by our language, by our culture, by concepts available to us, and by the history of how we've come to such truths. Take even the example of gravity. Our *description of* gravity has changed from Newton's "force" to Einstein's "curvature of spacetime." And

---

11. John 14:6a.

12. For example, McIntyre specifically argues that postmodernism led to our post-truth condition. See McIntyre, *Post-Truth*, 123–50.

13. Of course, postmodernism consists of widely diverse and differing positions and views, which defy easy generalizations. But this summary does encapsulate its key thesis, repeated in various ways among its proponents. For a comprehensive yet sympathetic overview of different postmodern theories regarding truth and reality, see Best and Kellner, *Postmodern Theory*.

this change required our prior theories and history of inquiry, as well as the specific concepts, language, and systems of measurement that were in place. And postmodernists would even add that the larger truths we value and collectively live by are often—if not always—selected and supported by those of us with power, based on what belief would benefit us from others believing such things.

For a postmodernist, our every description of reality, from scientific to superstitious, is thus like a *map*. There really *is* something that the map describes, such as the mountains and valleys, rivers and coastlines, roads and cities; it's not like they won't be there if we erase it from the map. But the maps are not some mirror images of these things. What's on our map are symbols and notations, made up and used by our culture. And there are different ways to draw the map; we could've used different symbols, and we can even select what to include in the map, and what to leave out. But the postmodern catch is: We can only ever see our maps, not the things that our maps represent.

Now, how far we can take this postmodernist argument is, of course, debatable. After all, can't some maps be *more true* than others? Can't a map be false, so that if you follow it, you'll become lost? But it does raise a very important point about truth: We can never completely take "us" out of the truths we hold.

And this confronts us with some disquieting questions. Can we ever *trust* our truth? After all, there are always things we miss, things we ignore, things we have yet to learn; there are always other sides, other ways to draw the map. In fact, how can we ever claim that *our* view of things is the *whole* truth? And are we using our map because it's true or because there are people profiting from its sales?

What about scientific truths though? Surely, they are beyond such challenges? But, even the most secure of our scientific truths can be overthrown tomorrow. Even more importantly, not even science is free from this human factor—from "us."

There's a widespread recognition today that findings in many currently published scientific studies cannot be consistently replicated; other scientists often cannot confirm whether a finding is true, and worse, they *do not try to*. This is called the "replication crisis," and the reasons for this crisis again turn out to be "us" and our all too *human* failings. Because scientists are just as susceptible to biases, conscious and unconscious, as everyone else; they can be just as negligent, making avoidable errors in methods and measurements. Nor are they above committing fraud by falsifying or fabricating data; and they're drawn, like the rest of us, to money, fame, and status. And our society rewards findings that are novel and sensational; it rarely cares for the slow, conscientious work that confirms whether the results really *are* true.[14] Simply put, if our search for truth is not motivated by the *love of* truth, not even science can be, well, *science*.

And this leads us back to Lonergan's transcendental precepts. Be attentive to everything. Seek understanding. Critically and thoroughly judge your ideas. Act with integrity. And above all, do these things because of *love*. This is the kind of *person* we must be to properly relate to reality and seek truth. If we can never separate "us" from the truths we find and hold, then our search for truth must first and foremost face "us"—*persons* with faults and failings. For it is a person that *draws our map*; it is a person that generates our truths.

And every truth is hearing God speaking.

TRUTH THAT GENERATES ALL OTHER TRUTHS IS OUR BEST ANALOGY OF GOD

All of reality—this entire speech-*like* reality and story-*like* history—is God "speaking." And so, every truth—our true description *of* reality and our true narrative *of* history—is us "hearing God speak." These are our *analogies* about Reality, for everything we say of God is an analogy.

Yet if we can never take "us" out of truths we hold, we can never escape who and what we are whenever we are trying to "hear God speak." *Our truth today may fail tomorrow; what's true here may not be true there*. And we need not adopt some postmodern skepticism to acknowledge this frailty of our truths.

But, even if we do, there is still one truth we can live by, even when all our other truths begin to fade. It is about what kind of person speaks forth new truths and renews our old truths. It is such *person* that connects us *to* Reality; it is such person that takes in the world around us, expanding our relation to reality and enriching our lives, beyond what we've known so far.

And we're drawn to such persons. This is why even those of us who have little interest in science are often fascinated by figures like Newton, Einstein, Darwin, or Hawking. It's why we're interested in what such people

---

14. For a deeper exploration of these human failings, which have compromised the practice of science, written by a scientist, see Ritchie, *Science Fictions*.

say about a number of different things, even when they're talking about things well outside their expertise. Which should strike us as odd. After all, a scientist who has made a profound discovery in cosmology can very well be terrible at knowing what's going on in their own lives, let alone at making fair judgments on social, political, or religious issues. But, this misdirected fascination is founded on our insight that persons are the conduit to every truth.

But who then *are* such persons?

To start with, such a person is *more* than some scientific genius who expands our collective knowledge. Because firstly, science does not deal with *all* the questions of truth; science is a subset of a wider way we engage reality, which was the insight of Lonergan. But a far more important reason is that scientific truths require more than some single, individual genius. For the strength of science comes from its piecemeal progress; "scientific knowledge" as a whole is actually like a giant puzzle, being put together by many people. So truth-seeking in science is both communal and personal; it depends on how we receive and impart truth *with other persons*.[15] But, many things can go wrong as truth moves between people: lies, negligence, and embellishments, from pride, envy, or greed.

So, the persons who lead us to truth and properly relate us to reality also reveal *relational* virtues. They would be attentive, seek understanding, and judge rationally. But they'd also *love*—love truth, love life, love justice, love mercy, love people. Otherwise, their motivation to reveal truth or do good would be suspect and easily become corrupted. They'd act with conviction, but be humble to hear corrections. They'd be courageous, speaking what needs to be spoken, yet patient and kind in speaking. And they'll be wise, to know which of these virtues are needed when.

It is this kind of person who will lead us to the most whole truth we can reach now in every circumstance and for every generation. Our truths today may become worn and lost tomorrow. And this can terrify us, since among the truths we can lose are the larger truths we live by now—truths that have kept us safe from becoming lost in a world that can hurt us. But the kind of person who leads us to such truth today will again lead us to such truth tomorrow. And *who* such persons are is itself a kind of truth—in

---

15. This communal and personal way science proceeds toward truth is described extensively by philosopher and chemist Michael Polanyi, in *Personal Knowledge*. His account is followed by T. S. Kuhn, who describes "normal science" as a collective "puzzle-solving" within a paradigm that is tacitly adopted by a community. See Kuhn, *Structure of Scientific Revolutions*, 30–39, 44.

fact, the most important truth. Because this is our enduring truth about what *generates all our truths*.[16]

And if every truth is "hearing God speaking," then such a person is *like* God speaking. This is partly what Christianity means by teaching that humanity is created in the "image of God."[17] Hearing this person speak is our closest possible approximation to hearing *God* "speaking" this speech-like reality and story-like history. The truths that such a person teaches us is God *accommodating* what is "being spoken" to us, in ways that we can understand today. Everything we say of God is an analogy, and such a person is our *best analogy* of God.

However, it need not be some *other* person who manifests God to us in this way. Because there are persons—voices—that speak within us. And in each of us, there's a voice that speaks our most truthful thoughts.

THE PERSON OF TRUTH THAT SPEAKS WITHIN US

Whenever we follow a voice—a particular side of us—that speaks within us, we also take on the character of that voice. An angry voice that howls for aggression; a wary voice that murmurs for prudence; a carefree voice asking for pleasure; fearful voice crying for retreat; a spiteful voice that seethes. We *become* more like them the more we follow what they demand.

Then, what about the voice of God? What is the *character* of that voice? What do we become when we follow what it speaks? And the answer is: the kind of person who leads us to the most whole truth we can speak now, with integrity and with love. This person is the character of that voice, and who you're turning into—the "truth" that generates our truths.

For postmodernism, our descriptions of reality are like maps. But for Christianity, its map of reality is a portrait of a *person*—one who connects us to the Person of Reality. For it is the character of that Person, and how that Person speaks, that the Christian Bible *maps* through its mosaic of

---

16. Peterson describes this kind of person as the mythical figure of the "Hero" whose creative exploration of the unknown defeats the forces of chaos and renews the world. It is the absence of this hero that makes the loss of our truths unbearable, pushing us to nihilism or its alter-ego, totalitarianism. And Peterson identifies this hero figure as the central figures in major religions today, such as the Buddha, and in the West, Christ—or in the terms of our book, the person that speaks what "God is speaking." See Peterson, *Maps of Meaning*, especially 19–20, 265–66, 382–84.

17. Gen 1:27.

life-stories. But to actually describe this Person, we'd need to journey together through that map, through its millennia-long story.

We can take a brief peek though, and glimpse the dim contours of what the Person of God that speaks within you will seem like, at least at first.

In a word, that Person will seem *like you*, but never quite you.

What does that mean? Well, though all of reality is God speaking, *your experience* of "God speaking" is bounded by *you*—bounded by your understanding, your limitations, and your character. That's the postmodern thesis. And if you are twisted, confused, or prone to lies, that will likewise distort, confuse, and deceive your very experience *of* Reality—how you experience God.

However, there's a better version of you. And it *is* a person. Because this "you" is a person you can at least conceive of becoming, one whose character relates to reality more properly. But this "you" is only *potentially* you. To become that person, you must heed its exhortations: be attentive; seek understanding; judge fairly; act with integrity; be courageous yet patient; have conviction but be humble; live with love. When you do, the reality you experience will become less distorted and deceitful, and more discernible and true.

But, this "you" is also *not* you. After all, if you fail to become this person, it will be that it was never you in the first place. Instead, this person you can become *beckons* to you, like a teacher—like someone going just a step ahead of you.

And no, this "you" is *not* your conscience, if by that you mean your "moral compass"—your internalization of how society judges what is right or wrong. Because this "you" is more than that; it is how *reality relates to you*. And reality can even reveal that your conscience is *wrong*, and this "you" can urge you to be better than that. For example, your conscience may clear you for publicly humiliating someone who "deserve it" by your society's collective judgment. But *this* "*you*" can question that judgment, beckoning you toward *greater* truth and love.

So, say you do heed this better "you," and step toward becoming that person, beyond your current self, and even your current conscience. This often will be a painful process; you'd need to genuinely face your faults and failings, and acknowledge some dark and ugly parts of you that you were trying to ignore. And you'd need to change, even if just a single step. If you do change, you'll become wiser, more truthful, and loving, so that your

There's truth, then there's truth that generates truths

experience of reality, your "hearing of God speaking," will become less limited, distorted, or deceitful.

However, when you do become this better "you," you'll find that there's *still* an even better you that's again beckoning and speaking to you those exhortations. And *this will always be the case*. This "you" will always be waiting in the next step of your life-journey, no matter where that is, speaking to you and beckoning you to follow. This "you" will beckon at your very worst, and will still beckon even at your unfailing best. This "you" will be like the horizon that's always further ahead as you journey toward it. And so, this "you" will *never actually be you*, but the one who will forever speak *to* you and guide you.[18]

God that speaks within us is the voice that speaks the truth. But we can never separate "us" from our truths. So, the Person of God within us accommodates to us by speaking *as* the person *we can become*, whoever we are, and speaking the most whole truth *we* can grasp now.

What Christians believe and confess, however, is that when we journey toward this horizon where this other "us" forever beckons, we'll find the person of Jesus Christ. We'll find that the *character* of this better "us," the *Person* of God that speaks within us, is the same as that of this man who lived two thousand years ago.

And our world crucified him, asking with a shrug, "What is truth?"

---

18. This process resembles what Jung called "individuation," and this "better you" that speaks the truth closely correlates with Jung's idea of the *Self*. For Jung, the "Self" is the complete potential of everything in you, both conscious and unconscious. But this Jungian Self is *not* you; "you" are your "Ego." And ego must relate to the Self as a guiding principle, because mistaking ego for the Self can lead to megalomania. And Jung identified the Self as what we'd experience, *psychologically*, as "God," and Christ as a representation of the Self. To explore his ideas further, see Jung, *Aion*, especially chapters 4–5.

PART THREE

What do you mean God is "good"?

CHAPTER NINE

Why would you think that God is "good"?

THERE ARE TIMES WHEN the order in which we ask our questions is important. Because some questions cannot even be asked properly, let alone be answered, without answering some prior questions. It's like trying to ask meaningful questions in an advanced algebra class when we haven't learned what *numbers* are; it's like sitting down to watch a movie that's nearing the end and asking who the person on the screen is, or why they're doing what they're doing. Or, it's like dropping into *this* chapter without reading the prior chapters of this book.

And the way we ask the questions regarding the "goodness" of God can often be this way. "Why do bad things happen if God is *good*?" "Why would a *good* God not get rid of evil?" These are very important questions—profound, even.[1] But, when I first began to *really* think about these questions, I realized that there were a couple of obvious questions that we should've asked first.

What do we mean by "good"?

And why would we even think that God is good in the first place?

---

1. There has been an interesting new development to this question, however. Yujin Nagasawa points out that evil poses a problem not only to traditional theists, but those who hold other worldviews too, *including atheists*; there's a mismatch between our expectation of a good reality and the actual world we live, and *everyone* has that mismatch, whether one believes in God or not. For details, see Nagasawa, *Problem of Evil for Atheists*, especially chapters 2, 7.

WHAT DO WE MEAN BY "GOOD"?

The problem with asking what we mean by "good" is that it covers a very *wide* range of things: Wayne Gretzky is "good" at ice hockey; Mother Theresa was a "good" person who cared for the poor; the Exoplanet K2-18b is a "good" candidate for hosting life. Then, which "good" are we speaking about here when we say that *God* is "good"?

Well, simply put: something that encompasses *all* of those meanings. Aquinas followed Aristotle by defining "Goodness" as essentially "what all desire," and argued that this "Goodness" is an aspect of "Being"—its "desirability."[2] So, the reason why we call our examples "good" is because they have something that is "desirable," though for very different reasons—to be good in some way is to be desirable in some way. Now, Aquinas obviously says much more than this, since we can just as easily say Cain "desired" to murder his brother Abel, which means murder is "good," at least for Cain. Nonetheless, it is a *good* starting definition if we want a more concrete grasp on what "goodness" means—see how this works?

God then is "good" in two ways. First, since God is the ground of being, God is the *source* of that desirability. Second, because God is the source of what we all desire, God is also what we desire the *most*, though we don't realize this because we don't truly know God.[3] So, the "goodness" of each and everything derives from the "goodness of God," *and* points toward it.

Except that all this is still really abstract, and "desire," just like "goodness," can be about so many different things. More to the point, what most of us today mean by saying that God is "good" is *moral* goodness. We tend to think of something like what Moses heard on the mountain after his people were freed from their enslavement in Egypt: God is "loving and kind," "compassionate and gracious," "patient, forgiving, yet just." So, how do these specific moral traits connect with our abstract definition of goodness as "desirability"? We may answer that such moral character is "desirable." But then, just what is that moral goodness desirable *for*?

Furthermore, religion and morality, since time immemorial, have been paired together. Societies and cultures across the world have drawn

---

2. Aquinas, *ST* I.q5.a1.

3. Aquinas, *ST* I.q6.aa1–3; see also *ST* I.q2.a1.ad1, I.q6.a2. This desirability of God is a central theme of Augustine's writings, summed up by his praise to God: "You have made us for yourself, and our hearts are restless until they rest in you" (*Confessions* 1.1). This is also why Hart describes God as Being, Consciousness, *and* Bliss. See Hart, *Experience of God*, 238–51.

their moral rules and practices from their religious teachings, believing that their gods judge their lives and actions. In that particular respect at least, Christians are no different; they believe that God is their judge because God is *morally good*. But, what does this mean, really?

In this book, we've translated the Christian idea of "God" as "Reality," and more specifically, "all of reality" as "God speaking." What then would it mean to say that "God is good"? Because we'd be saying "Reality is good"—*morally* good—and that "all of reality" is *loving* and *kind*, *patient* yet *just*. What could *that* possibly mean?

And again, to really answer that question meaningfully, we'd need to journey through the vast mosaic of life-stories that the Bible recounts. After all, moral goodness is the character of the *Person* of God. And that character—the character of Reality—is what those whose lives compose that mosaic *experienced*, both from that inner voice of truth that spoke with them and how reality around them then unfolded.

However, even their stories did not start from a blank-slate. It's not like Abraham, for example, seriously believed that the God who first spoke to him was *evil*, and then was stunned to find out that he was wrong. Which brings up this question: Why would anyone think that God is—*Reality* is—good in the first place? Morally good, I mean? After all, there are plenty of things that happen in our world that would lead us to think that Reality is *evil*, or at least amoral.

WHAT DOES IT MEAN TO SAY SOMETHING IS MORALLY GOOD?

First though, what *is* morality? What is good and what is evil? What is right and what is wrong? These are perennial questions that we have yet to fully answer. However, we can at least answer *why* those questions arise, in regard to human beings in any case. And it again has to do with a particular feature of our speech-like reality. To be specific, it has to do with the fact that there are many possible ways that our reality can unfold, from many possible actions that we can take.

So, say, you're running through a park, because there's a shortcut to where you'll have your job interview, but then you see an elderly man, collapsed on the ground. Should you help this person? But if you do, you won't make the interview in time, and you *really* want this job. Maybe there's someone else who can help? But you don't see anyone else nearby. So, what do you do?

You are now faced with a choice of how you can make things unfold from here. You can ignore that person and go to your interview, hoping that someone else will come along. You can help him, possibly giving up on that job you wanted. You can even pick his wallet, pocket his cash, *and then* go to your interview. And your choice implies you have ascribed relative *value* to the different actions you can take, and what that'll unfold. Asking what is the "good" thing to do here, in an important way, is asking which of those holds the greatest value—or, which is the most "desirable." Is helping this stranger in trouble *more desirable* than getting your dream job? Is adding to your personal wealth *more desirable* than the well-being of some stranger? And *why*? Why is one action and what it unfolds more desirable than some others? And desirable for whom?

That "why" and "for whom" is the question that has troubled ethicists and moral philosophers for the past several centuries; we can't quite come up with a satisfying answer. However, here's one very influential answer, which was put forth about forty-five years ago by a philosopher named Alasdair MacIntyre. Examining ancient and medieval works, he came to conclude that how we ascribed values to these actions—how we reasoned about morality and ethics—was based on a larger vision of our place and life in this world.[4]

So, this how it works: Let's say, you're a student, and your goal *as* a student is to get all A's in your courses—because is there really any other grade? If *that* is how you envision your life and set up your goals, the actions you ought to take—actions that are more "desirable" for you in that context—are the ones that will reach your goal to get those A's. So, reviewing your notes the night before your exam is far more desirable than partying with your friends, because it enables you to become that A student. Skipping your exam is outright *un*desirable, as it will utterly derail your goals. In a similar way, moral actions are actions that are desirable because they'll bring forth the kind of world that we're *aiming for*—the world we, again, *desire*. But, what kind of world is that? Simply put, it is the world in which humanity *flourishes*.

But, what does it mean for us to flourish, really? If all of us live a life of perpetual luxury, while say, our planet dies, are we flourishing? Or, if we make ninety-nine people live an ideal life, by making one person live in

---

4. For the details of this argument, see MacIntyre, *After Virtue*.

perpetual torment, are we flourishing? Or, if every single one of us is given a life of ease and comfort, but because of that, we no longer strive to learn, grow, and explore, are we flourishing?

What does it mean for humanity to flourish? We're still working on that question even now. But we do know a few things about what it means for us to *not* flourish. For example, we cannot flourish if we are all dead. And we probably aren't flourishing if we are making each other suffer pointlessly. Of course, our world has its share of suffering and pain, and plenty of it, but it's another thing entirely if we make each other suffer for no other reason than, say, spite and malice.

All this is very much in tune with the modern, evolutionary account of our morality as well. According to that view, humanity evolved morality because it was adaptive for our survival. But how can this be? After all, isn't evolution about the survival of the fittest, where the strong survives and the weak perishes? Yet, our morality calls us to protect the weak among us, and we hold great respect for those who put their lives on the line for the sake of others.

Well, according to evolutionary accounts, our morality—based on altruism, social cooperation, and mutual trust—makes us strong *as a species*.[5] I mean, consider what would happen if you were suddenly left alone in an uninhabited wilderness, and the only things you had with you were things you made from scratch by yourself—which for most of us would mean *nothing at all*. Other people—people who make things, discover things, teach us things, our family, friends, civilization—is what has enabled us to survive and flourish. We can even say, if we're feeling more sentimental, our "*love*" for each other is what makes *all* of humanity strong *together*.

So, what happens if we lie, cheat, steal, or even kill other people to get ahead? Well, those actions may benefit some of us in the short term. But they will ultimately undermine what holds us together and makes us stronger, leaving every one of us vulnerable and unable to flourish. You can even expand on this to include environmental ethics. We've always known that everything is interconnected; but now we know that things in our world are even more closely interdependent than we've imagined.

---

5. One widely known version of this evolutionary account of human morality is presented by Richard Dawkins. He argued that altruistic actions and cooperation can evolve if they enable our *genes* to survive—either related genes in our relatives, by helping them, or our own genes, by facilitating future reciprocation. This account is also noteworthy to our efforts to translate "God" for our Godless world because it's from a vocally atheist perspective. See Dawkins, *Selfish Gene*.

Exploiting our environment for profit may benefit *some* of us in the short term, but *all* of us will suffer in the long term. So, humanity has evolved actions or practices that enable us to *flourish together* in the long term, or at least avoid mutual destruction; that's what led to our moral sense of right and wrong.

FROM MORALITY AND THE GODS TO GOD AND OUR MORAL REALITY

I think this dynamic of "flourishing," to which our morality aims, is what underlies the ancient belief across the world that the gods judge humanity for their actions. Humanity encountered their gods in the voices that called them to particular kind of actions. And different kinds of actions shaped their world in different ways; some led their society to flourish and prosper, while others pulled it apart and destroyed it. This dynamic is partly why people viewed their gods not as mere inner personas but as the powers and forces that shape their world. So, the gods that ancient societies tended to worship were those that stood for things that made their society flourish—gods identified with order rather than chaos, moral virtues rather than vices. And when a society followed the call of those gods—to speak the truth, act justly, and cooperate with each other—it was usually rewarded with order, stability, and even prosperity. On the other hand, when society was deceitful, unjust, violent, and treacherous, it was punished with destruction, or at least slow degradation. And in that sense, gods seemed to uphold moral order and judge human beings for their moral acts.[6]

But then, what about the idea of God? After all, "God" is not "god."

There's this belief in many different ancient cultures, that there is a moral order that *even the gods had to follow*. This order, in turn, was an aspect of the larger, *cosmic* order, exemplified by the orderly movements of the heavens—the sun, moon, and the stars—and the cycles of seasons, and of life itself. So, just as there is order in the cosmos, there is order in how the gods rule the world, and how humans are to live and organize their society.

---

6. This kind of account regarding the relation between morality and the gods leads to how it'd then be structured into a society and culture, which is an established theme in sociological theories regarding religion. A founding work on this is by Emile Durkheim, who viewed religion as the most fundamental social institution of humanity, so that moral practices that a society collectively lived by were projected onto the entities in its sacred domain—such as its gods. To explore his ideas further, see Durkheim, *Elementary Forms of Religious Life*.

Why would you think that God is "good"?

And this is a very, *very* old idea. In ancient Egypt, for example, this order was called *Ma'at*, which held together its concepts of truth, balance, morality, and law. The ancient Egyptians believed that when the gods brought forth order out of chaos in the creation of the cosmos, or when human beings lived morally and their kings ruled so that their society flourished, they were all doing so according to the principle of Ma'at. There's a similar idea in ancient India and its oldest religious text, the *Rigveda*, written between three to four thousand years ago. It teaches that the entire cosmos is ordered by the principle it calls *Rta*, which represents again the concepts of truth, law, and sacrifice. It is this Rta that regulates and coordinates everything in the cosmos; the gods have their powers by upholding this order, while human beings manifest Rta through their moral living and proper religious rituals. And in ancient China, from three thousand years ago or so, there was the idea that the entire cosmos unfolds according to *Tian-Ming*, which means, the "Will of Heaven." This "Will" manifest itself in the order and the cycle of changes in Nature, and it was this "Will" that upholds human rulers who are benevolent and lead their people to flourish. But, this same "Will" also repudiates rulers whose moral failures make their people suffer, and this is what justifies people in deposing their ruler.[7]

Now, these aren't just some old ideas that have disappeared in our modern day. I mean, consider the core claim of these beliefs. There is order and laws to the cosmos; and *all* of us live *in this order*. And this order has structured this world in such a way that if we want to flourish as a people, we need to seek truth rather than indulge in falsehood, and act in ways that will establish trust, good will, and order among us. If we do not, our society will unravel into distrust, violence, and chaos, where none of us will flourish. Our modern, *scientific* understanding of the universe, and our evolutionary account of human society and morality, if anything, simply presents a complex and developed version of this very *same* idea.

What of God though? Well, these old ideas regarding *Ma'at*, *Rta*, *Tian-Ming*, and so on, pointed to something that is higher and more primordial than the gods—to something like a supreme being. And such

---

7. For an in-depth exploration of these concepts, as they are embedded into ancient religious thought and mythic worldviews, see Eliade, *History of Religious Ideas*, vols. 1–2. Mircea Eliade was a highly influential historian and scholar, whose work described the patterns and structures of religious experience across cultures, and how it has shaped humanity's understanding of reality. We need not explore his specific ideas for our translations of "God" in this book, but they remain paradigmatic, if partly contested, to the field of religious studies today.

ideas then developed into more complex and unified versions through the philosophical discourses of later eras. They became the ideas about the principle of reality, which structures and defines all things and how they come to be, including our morality. One such idea, in Greek philosophy, was that of the *Logos*. And we've previously explored how this Logos is the founding principle of modern science, as well as what the Jews and the Christians identify as the very *Speech* of God—"God *speaking*."

So, in Christianity, this cosmic order, which even the gods must follow, the principle that structures and governs the universe, is "God speaking." And these structures that God is "speaking" are such that those who seek and speak truth, act justly, and live with love, flourish together.

WHAT IT MEANS TO SAY THAT "GOD IS GOOD" IF "GOD" IS "REALITY"

We can now return to our first question: What does it mean to say that "God is good"?

When we imagine "God" as some Super-Zeus entity *in* our reality, we tend to understand the "goodness" of this "God" in the following way: This entity decreed to us our moral laws based on his moral goodness. And his "goodness" obliges this entity to stop any evil and suffering from happening in our world. After all, if *we* had his powers and *we* are good, then we'd do the same. This entity, in that sense, is a combination of a celestial lawgiver and Superman. But our Godless world is painfully aware that this entity has been absent from his job. For we've waited in vain for him to swoop in and stop the evils that happen in our world. Where then is this entity, and how can this entity be "good"?

However, our translations of "God" so far place us in a very different frame and question altogether. "God" is not an entity in our reality; God *is Reality*. All of reality is "God speaking"—reality that's all around us, with which we are immediately engaged. And so, saying that "God is good," is not about the moral qualities of some hypothetical entity in some higher level of our reality, who's yet to show himself; it's about the very character *of* reality *in which* we live now.

And this reality unfolds in particular ways in response to what we do, which seems to be the basis of our morality. Now, I've heard some people say in popular conversations that morality is just rules that our society has set down, which pointedly ignores the question of why a society would set such rules in the first place. And the answer is: These rules are approximations of which kind of actions lead us, humanity, to flourish together, and which lead us to perish together. I say, "approximations," because we are still trying to get it right—and sometimes we may even sneak in false rules that'll let some of us manipulate others and hold power over them. But, at its basis, it's about what will make us flourish or perish together. I mean, just imagine what would happen if *everyone*, to their best ability, lived by truthfulness, justice, and love, and compare that with what would happen if everyone instead lived by deception, injustice, and malice. And that question becomes even more urgent in our world today, in which every one of us is connected by trade and communication, and our nations are armed with *weapons of mass destruction*.

But if we, as a species or as a society, will likely perish by deception, injustice, and malice, and likely thrive by truthfulness, justice, and love, then a rather interesting sort of evolutionary selection emerges. And it's a selection that leads to *propagation of traits that are moral*—sort of like "memes."[8] Simply put, things like deception, injustice, and malice will eventually destroy themselves along with those who perish by them; but, truthfulness, justice, and love will propagate along with those who flourish because of them. If so, our reality is structured so that moral virtues, or *goodness*, is what will live on and thrive—*if* we as a society ever live by it. And *that reality* is "God speaking."[9]

Reality is speech-like. And God is like a "speaker" in that there are infinite other realities that could've been "spoken" instead. Yet the reality that *is* being spoken is one that "selects" goodness; it is one where goodness flourishes and evil perishes. *That* is God is speaking; that is the history that

---

8. The term, "meme" is again from Dawkins, who argued that just as genes propagate and replicate in response to selective pressures, cultural ideas and practices can do so as well. See Dawkins, *Selfish Gene*, 192. But, my point is somewhat different. I don't just mean that morality is a cultural replicator, propagating in the meme pool of human cultures; I mean that it propagates *because* it enables humanity as a whole, when it practices it, to survive.

9. As to *exactly* what these moral structures would be, and what they imply regarding the moral character of God, remains an open question. One recent, comprehensive proposal was presented by theologian Nancey Murphy, and cosmologist George F. R. Ellis. Based on their analysis of the relation between the fields of sciences, ethics, and theology, they present a moral universe that reflects their Christian anabaptist faith in God, centered on self-sacrifice and nonviolence. Theirs is just one possible account though, based on very specific cosmological, sociological, and ethical positions. See Murphy and Ellis, *Moral Nature of the Universe*, especially 15–18, and chapters 5–6, 8–9.

God is unfolding. And that is what the people in the Bible heard God speak personally *to* them:

> See, I set before you today life and prosperity, death and destruction. For I command you today to love [Yahweh], your God, to walk in obedience to him, and to keep his commands, decrees and laws; then you will live and increase, and [Yahweh], your God will bless you in the land you are entering to possess.[10]

And that is what it meant to say that "God is good," even before that long journey across the generations that the Bible recounts. It was from that starting point that the people in the Bible then experienced and mapped the personal character of Reality that spoke with them.

GOODNESS IS WHAT GOD IS SPEAKING TO US

But, does goodness actually flourish and evil really perish? After all, evil seems alive and well in our world.

This question, however, does not actually grasp the truly *terrifying* implication of what it means to say that "God is good." Because the *contest* between goodness and evil is still *ongoing* as far as we, humanity, are concerned. Reality is such that goodness will flourish and evil will perish, yes, but what *is* certain for us in that formulation is only that *evil will perish*. For goodness will flourish only if that is what we—*all of us*—live by, together. And we are nowhere near there yet. And if our world is filled with evil—if lies, injustice, and malice are what come to characterize all our actions—we *will* destroy each other and perish together. "Together" seems to be the key point here. We rise *and* fall together, like it or not.

That's how it is. We are vulnerable to other people's wrongs—to their hurtful words, their lies and betrayals, their violence. We live with our society's wrongs—its corruption and disinformation, its injustices and wars. And this often leads us to do the same; we'll hurt others or deceive them, or strive to be the ones that benefit from these injustices, rather than to be those who are victimized.

And if this leads all of us closer to perishing together, we may decry that this is unfair. After all, we didn't *start* it. Why is it that we're so deeply affected by what *other people* do? So, we may say: If this is how reality is

---

10. Deut 30:15–16 (NIV).

Why would you think that God is "good"?

structured and unfolds, and *that* is "God speaking," then surely God is not good!

But, I notice that we rarely say the same for the opposite. Other people also do good things, which affect us. The reason why you can even read this book, not exposed to the elements, with the lights on, and food available—is because of other people. And it's no use saying that you've paid for these things with money; if there were no other people to begin with, no amount of money will get you these things. And our lives are made worthwhile *by* other people—people who love us and people we love. Just as other people hurt us, other people hold us up. Things we learn, things that protect us, things that enrich our lives, are from other people; none of them were brought about by us. But, we don't say any of *this* is unfair.

All of us are connected, so that the good things we do bless not only us but others too—even those we've never met. Our connectedness amplifies what we do far beyond what each of us can do alone. This is why we can make progress; we don't start from scratch; we build upon what others have done. That is how we raised up civilizations. And what would our world be like if the things we had done so far had always been—or even just mostly been—good, and all of them had amplified each other?

Yet, what amplifies the good can also amplify the bad. We can be blessed not only by the things we've done but also by things others have done; and so, we can be cursed in the same way, not only by things we've done but also by things others have done.

For whatever reason, our reality seems to be structured to maximize *not* the *actuality* of good things, but their *potentiality*. It's as if we're still in the midst of a long journey, in which the full "goodness" of reality is still unfolding. And *that* is "God speaking."

Again, this is nowhere near the full meaning of what Christianity means by "God is good." And despite what it may have seemed, none of this really answers the question of suffering and evil. After all, if God is the "Speaker" that could've spoken infinite other speech-like realities, or at least unfolded a different history, could God not have spoken and unfolded something else? A reality that did not have the suffering that ours has? One in which a mass-murdering dictator had a change of heart just a few years earlier? Or one in which that wildfire or tsunami or earthquake did not happen, or struck somewhere uninhabited?

This book, however, will go no further regarding these questions, and not just because they defy simple answers.[11] *We just aren't there yet* on our journey. And a proper answer would not only be reached by reason but will be *felt* and *experienced*. Not to mention that we aren't going into topics like heaven or hell or the final judgment, which would also be part of such answers. What we're doing here is translation; that's why we've been asking what it even *means* to say that "God is good" in the first place. So, when we do wrestle with the question of evil and the goodness of God, we'd have the vocabulary to do so.

But, we're not yet finished with our translations. For God's "goodness" is about more than just how our reality is structured. God is Reality, but this Reality also personally speaks *to us*, accommodating to *our* level of understanding and ability wherever and whenever we are. And the Person of God that has been speaking within us is even now beckoning us away from evil and toward good. That inner contest too is still ongoing, as we continue to journey toward a world where we'll flourish together. And that contest is as perilous as it is worthwhile.

---

11. There *are* some thoughtful and nuanced answers. For a recent theological critique against facile answers to explain away suffering, while passionately affirming God's opposition to it, see Hart's *Doors of the Sea*; for an influential, contemporary answer to the *logical* problem of evil, see Plantinga's *God, Freedom, and Evil*; Murphy and Ellis also presents their answer in *Moral Nature of the Universe*, chapter 10.

CHAPTER TEN

Why the idea of sin and judgment still haunts us

World Peace. Almost everyone would agree that it's a good thing. So, why don't we have it?

A simple answer is: Because *no one* really *wants world peace.*

Now, most people do genuinely wish for their world to be without conflict, but that's not quite the same thing. Because conflicts have reasons—there are prejudices, interests, and grievances at play—and peace, true peace that addresses those reasons, has a price. It requires dialogue and understanding, compromise and cooperation, reconciliation and trust, all of which have costs, and *risks*. And it will demand actions we'd rather not do. We may need to give up our privileges; we may need to acknowledge our past wrongs and make restitutions; we may need to forgive, while recognizing that some wrongs can never fully be made right. And almost no one wants to pay such a price—especially when there's no guarantee that others would pay their share. And so, our generation will continue to war, as did our parents, as will our children, and our world will never know peace.

And according to Christianity, *that* is the pattern of our sin and the nature of the judgment upon us.

THE IDEA OF "SIN" AND WHY WE STUMBLE OVER IT TODAY

Our speech-like reality is a *moral* reality. And I'd contend that this moral character of reality is as real as any law of Nature—as real as the principles of evolution and natural selection. Because we are the kind of creatures that *will* perish together if our world becomes filled with deceit, injustice, and malice. This is especially true in our connected, globalized world with its nuclear weapons; but even without that, a treacherous and violent society would either collapse on its own or make too many enemies. And how we perish, or flourish, can unfold through generations, just like the process of evolution. That is how we humans are. And it's no use pointing out that this moral dynamic of our world applies only to creatures like humanity, and not to some wider physical reality. Every law of Nature requires a specific condition to operate: principles of evolution require life; laws of chemistry require atoms; even gravity requires matter. And *all* such laws are part of the *Logos*—"God speaking"—as is this moral structure of our human world.

It is in such reality that the ideas of "sin" and "judgment" confront us. Christianity and its message is deeply concerned with this subject. A large portion of its worship, ceremonies, and rites are intertwined with it, with the call to repentance—which is to acknowledge one's sin and turn away from it—and the proclamation that God has forgiven our sins.

But *what is* "*sin*"? How are we to translate this idea for our Godless world? Whenever the word is mentioned today, what many of us tend to imagine is some caricature of a Bible-waving preacher, telling us that we'll be "punished" for the bad things we did. And this is not just about how all of us can perish *together* because of what we're doing; it's about how *each of us*, our *individual* lives and actions, will be judged by God. But leaving aside the obvious question of whether that actually happens, here and now or in some afterlife, what specific things are so bad that we should be punished for them—by "God," no less?

And this is where our rather general exploration so far about the "moral reality" that God is "speaking" collides with a practical problem. What things, *specifically*, is our moral reality structured *against*? So, deceit, injustice, and malice will lead us to perish together, yes, but what really *counts as those*? For example, what makes a society unjust? And not just unjust, but *so unjust* that it will collapse, taking us down with it? Which law? Which form of economy? Which social system? And what can each of us possibly do that would actually make a difference? And which of *those* would be so bad as to deserve some kind of *punishment*?

Well, what do *we* think are the kind of things people should be punished for today? Again, that's hard to say. Because there are two problems in trying to answer this question.

The first is that we tend to value freedom nowadays, especially in the West, so we're reluctant to identify the things people shouldn't do, let alone those they should be punished for. Now, we usually seem to draw the line at causing physical harm; so, we agree that something like that should be punished. Yet, most of us don't go out of our way to hurt people for no good reason; we aren't *malevolent*, or so we'd like to think. And so, we may feel that this talk of sin and judgment does not, or at least *should not*, apply to us. It should only apply to violent criminals and such.

But, the idea of "sin" seems to point to something more, something which implicates all of us. Well, there's sex. Things Christianity says about sins regarding sex seem to apply to a lot more people than outright violence and malevolence. And maybe that's why in popular culture, Christians are so often depicted as obsessed with the topic. Except that something like, say, sex outside marriage, is no longer seen as wrong in our society. And we'd struggle to understand why *that* would be grave enough that it'd need punishments from God.

These examples illustrate our two problems when we try to identify *specific things* as "sin." Things that most of us would actually agree as something that deserves punishment are usually too narrow in scope to fit the wider Christian idea of "sin." But, for anything more, we have trouble understanding why *that* deserves punishment.

And I think a significant reason for this is because we tend to understand moral standards today as largely relative to the specific cultures and times of the people who live by them. So, is something a sin if it is considered a moral wrong in one society yet is permitted in another?

Of course, there *are* some moral principles that everyone seems to agree on across cultures and times. But these, again, tend to be so general that people will disagree on how they ought to be applied. So, while we'll agree on principles like "do no harm" or "be fair and just," we again face questions over the specifics. What is being fair and just? Is capitalism more fair than socialism? Will society be more just when run by conservatives, or progressives? And what defines harm? Can a political comment harm?

Is not joining climate activism causing harm? Or is causing harm ever justified? If so, when?

And even when people do agree on something more specific, their agreement tends to set a really low bar. Physical violence is bad—except of course, we can justify violence toward those who "deserve it." So, violence against innocent people is bad—except who gets to set the standard of innocence? If an entire people are suffering under an apartheid regime, are the ordinary citizens who empowered that regime "innocent"? If, on the other hand, that oppressed people group has fostered or encouraged its members to commit acts of mass terrorism, are they "innocent"? And considering how nations, governments, and peoples even today use such reasoning to justify indiscriminate killings, we know bars can always be lowered.

So, what then is sin? Where in that spectrum of moral wrongs should we find it?

Perhaps the Bible will tell us. And it does. But if we think it will simply give us a list of clear moral rights and wrongs, dos and don'ts for today, we may be disappointed. Some seem clear enough at first; there's the Ten commandments. Except, of course, a secular society won't keep the first four—no other gods, no idols, no taking the Lord's name in vain, keep the sabbath, and the like. And while we may nod in agreement on "thou shalt not murder," well again, what defines murder—a wrongful killing? Is capital punishment wrong? What about war? Euthanasia? And while we may still frown at adultery, it's no longer a crime.

And the problem is compounded because the moral standard in the Bible—in the Christian Old Testament, for example—is that of the Iron-Age civilization of ancient Israel. And what we consider morally right or wrong—such as slavery—has gone through some changes in the last three thousand years. All of this adds to the question of how to make sense of this old idea of "sin" in our Godless world.

"SIN" AS "MISSING THE MARK," IN OUR WORLD OF POSSIBILITIES

Our questions so far, however, indicate why we keep stumbling over the idea of sin and judgment; it's because we tend to understand it purely in *judicial terms*—as punishment for some crime. Now, this is one model—one

Why the idea of sin and judgment still haunts us

analogy—of what's going on, and I'd even say the main one.[1] But again, there are always limits to our analogies about reality, and they often require other analogies to calibrate our understanding.

Christian theology has developed other analogies about sin. One describes sin as something like a disease, which plagues all humanity. Another describes it as a kind of power that holds us captive or hostage. Both describe "sin" as a kind of condition that is imposed over all of us, which will lead us to our destruction and death, unless we are healed or rescued.[2] So, to understand this idea of "sin," especially in regard to our translations of "God," we'll need a larger definition—one that points to something more fundamental to how we live, encompassing not just its moral and penal aspect, but its nature as a common human condition. And I think that even today, we are still deeply haunted by what the Christian idea of sin and judgment was trying to express—and haunted in a way that I suspect we can't quite fully grasp, precisely because we think we've cast aside such outdated notions.

The Greek word for "sin" in the New Testament is "*hamartia*," which means "to miss the mark," or more generally to fail some standard in some way. This was how the word was translated from the Hebrew Bible, which had a number of other words for "sin" as well, including "rebellion," "transgression," "perversity," and others.[3] We'll touch on these other meanings elsewhere, but the question for this chapter is: *What's the mark* that we're supposedly missing?

---

1. After all, in the Christian Old Testament, to break any of the laws that God spoke to Moses is considered "sin," and the apostle Paul discusses sin in terms of laws and judgment in Romans 2:1–16; Aquinas also quotes and confirms Augustine, by defining sin as "word, deed, or desire contrary to the eternal law" of God. However, "laws" seem to mean more than just a penal code, since Aquinas then describes "eternal laws" as "God's reason, so to speak," which this book has identified as the *Logos*, or "God speaking." Aquinas, *ST* I-II.q71.a6.

2. These analogies too have their biblical basis. It is by the wounds of God's chosen one that we are "healed" (Isa 53:5) and the main ministry of Jesus during his lifetime was that of healing. The apostle Paul also speaks of sin as something like being enslaved (Rom 6:12–23; 7:7–25). For a concise summary of the different analogies of sin in Christian theology, see McGrath, *Christian Theology*, 329–32.

3. A prominent and frequent Hebrew word, which connected to the Greek "*hamartia*" was "*hātā*," meaning "miss the mark." But, there were other significant words. One such word was "*pesha*," meaning "rebellion" or "transgression," which pointed to the relational aspect of sin. There was also "*āwon*," meaning "perversity" or "inequity," describing the twisted or crooked nature of sin.

Perhaps, we can think about it in terms of *possibilities*. There are many different ways our lives could have unfolded and can still unfold. There are many ways that things could've happened differently, and many ways things may yet happen. We've explored how our moral questions arise because of this character of our reality.

This also points us back to a key point in our translations of "God" as "Reality." Reality is not only about what *is*, but about an infinite possibility of what *can be*. And that's one meaning of the Hebrew phrase that the name of God in the Bible, "Yahweh," points to, in how it can be translated as "I will be who I will be," or as "I cause to be whatever I cause to be." So, as we engage reality—as we interact with God, the "I will be who I will be"—there's an unlimited array of possibilities that can unfold.

And *some possibilities are worse than others*.

Here's a simple way of putting it, in the form of a question: Is the world we're living in the best possible world we could've made it? And is your life the best that you could've made of it?

Now, immediately, this raises a difficult question: What would the "best" world look like, exactly? What would the "best" life be like? Is our idea of the best world, or best life, even a correct one, assuming we can coherently and clearly imagine one?

So, let me revise the question so that it's more modest: Could our world have been *better*? Not best—whatever that looks like. Just, better than it is now? Could your life have been better? Not only is that more answerable, the general direction to what's "better" is clear in the Christian perspective.

THE QUESTIONS THAT THE PERSON OF LOVE POSES TO US

There's a verse in the Bible that people often quote, including this book: "God is Love." But, why "Love"? After all, there are other words—other analogies—to describe God, to characterize *all* of reality as a whole. Why "love" specifically? Well, it's because just as what connects us to our speech-like reality is the person that speaks the truth, what connects us to our *moral* reality is the person that *loves*—and both are God "speaking" to us.

Morality, which aims for human flourishing, is founded on *love*. Love makes our flourishing *desirable*, which is to say, "*good*." What else but a love of life, including our own, would make us *want* to flourish in the first place? What else but love of others would motivate us to flourish *together*?

Our specific ethical rules or precepts may change over time and vary by culture, but our *personal reason* for formulating every such precept *is love*—love of life, love of others, love of our society. This is what the Christian Bible is pointing out when the apostle Paul writes, "For the entire law is fulfilled in keeping this one command: 'Love your neighbor as yourself.'"[4] The many laws found in the Bible, some of which seem strange to us today, were specific ways that people of that time and culture tried to fulfill this principle of love.

And so, our best analogy of God "speaking" a *moral* reality in which we can flourish is the person who leads us all toward a moral life *because they love*. The character of such person also points to the *Person* of Reality that speaks *to us* what is "good"—the Person of God. And a better version of ourselves that this Person is always beckoning us to is the one that loves *more*.

And we intuitively know that "love" is key to how we are to relate to reality as a whole. Think about it. Say, your life is the following: you love the people around you—you love your family, your relatives, your friends, your co-workers and neighbors; and you love your town, your home, your country, and you love your job, your livelihood, your hobbies; you love the forests, mountains, and seas, the sun, the moon, and the starry sky, and the wonders of the world around you. And you love yourself. This isn't to say there won't be pain or suffering beyond your control. But a life in which you love like this would be *worth* living—worth the pain.

Conversely, say you hate your family, your relatives, whom you have to see on holidays; you hate your so-called friends, your co-workers and your neighbors; you hate your town, your society; you hate your job, your livelihood, your boring hobbies; you couldn't care less about Nature, or the ugly world. And you hate yourself. What would living *that* life be like? Even if there's no physical pain or suffering, wouldn't this hate-filled life be *hell* on earth? And indeed, *hell* in Christianity is defined precisely as that "place"—for lack of better words—where God, who *is* Love, is irreversibly shut out of your life forever.

So, now that we have an idea of the direction toward a better world, we can ask: Could our world be better than it is? We may not know what a perfect world would look like, but we can still ask, whether our world could've been *more loving* than it is now—more kind, more just, more caring. Could it have been a world where people loved each other more in real

---

4. Gal 5:14 (NIV); see also Rom 13:8–10; 1 Cor 13.

and concrete ways, looked after each other, and derived joy and meaning because they did so? Could we have made our world better?

And if the answer is yes, the question is—and it is a question from that very voice of truth that beckons to us: *Why isn't it that way now?*

Could your life have been better? Could it have been where you loved it more? Loved the people around you more? Loved what you're doing more, doing what you believe is meaningful, and doing so truthfully and with integrity? Could your life be better?

And if yes, the question is again: *Why isn't it that way now?*

Perhaps, there were factors and forces beyond our control. But then, given our limitations, could our world, and our lives, have been better? Could we have made them better with what we had then? A place we love more? What about now?

And if yes, the question still is: *Why isn't it that way now?*

Because *that* is the mark that we have missed.

THE "WHY" IS OUR SIN

The "Why" is important.

We usually know all too well *why* we missed the mark, why everything is *not* what it could have been or can be. We may not know clearly, but we know enough. And this "why" can include something truly horrific; acts of sheer malice and spite, demeaning or hurting others, simply because we can. Sometimes we *know* something to be wrong, and even know it'd make our world worse, but we don't care—or we even *like* that it will. This is the aspect of "perversity" in one of the words in the Bible for "sin."[5] This perversity may include something seemingly insignificant though, such as treating your co-workers less patiently than you could have, or ignoring the plight of someone you could've helped. They all add up though—a life and world that could've been better, a possibility that was within your grasp, but was lost with your full knowledge.

Now, some of why our world is worse than it could have been may be due to honest mistakes; we may not have known better. But the voice that speaks the truth to us can be relentless against our self-serving excuses.

---

5. A key point in Christian theology regarding sin is that it is not merely due to some lack of knowledge of what is good, but a kind of "perverseness of will." Some notable examples are Augustine's analysis of the will and Calvin's doctrine of human depravity and the bondage of the will. See Augustine, *Confessions*, 2.4; Calvin, *Institutes*, 2.3-4.

Couldn't we have known better? Were there no signs we could've given greater attention to? Were there no voices of warning that were ignored?

There has been real scientific disagreement in the past over whether smoking causes cancer, or whether human-made climate change is happening, or whether wearing masks offers protection against the COVID-19 pandemic. And the harm has been unfolding even while we argued. We may say that we couldn't have known at the time what was going on. But, did we really reach the right conclusion as quickly as we could have? Or were there things we chose not to notice, any data we ignored, or concerns we dismissed? We've already explored how our *moral* failings can distort the very practice of seeking truth.

And if we were to delve deeper into our inner motivations—things no one but ourselves can know about, yet what that Person of truth points us to—the question becomes sharper. If we failed to find the truth, if we missed some data, or dismissed some early warnings, *why* did we? Aside from all the self-justifications we can make, what *really* made us miss them? Inconvenience? Complacency? *Arrogance?*

Now, none of these are the kind of things that will convict you in court. But they are what Christianity identifies as "sin": our character, our heart, which led us to miss the mark. And the world we live in is the result of it.

But, there's even more to how our sins shape our world, because according to Christianity, "sin" is inherited.[6] Let's take our environmental crisis, for example. The result of us missing the mark—the environmental degradation, climate change, polluted waters and oceans—are passed down; we live with its consequences. But more importantly, the *practices* and *habits* we formed that led to our crisis today are also passed down. The reliance we developed yesterday for fossil fuels, plastic waste, and unchecked consumerism has become the *norm* today, and to change that now would incur a painful cost.

Here's another example. Say, some political leaders start resorting to lies, incitement, and bribery to gain more power today. Their rivals then

---

6. The idea that sin can be inherited, based on the doctrine known as "original sin," has been central to Christian theology. It is based on biblical passages such as the following: "Therefore, just as sin entered the world through one man, and death through sin, and in this way death came to all people, because all sinned" (Rom 5:12), or "Surely I was sinful at birth, sinful from the time my mother conceived me" (Ps 51:5). Augustine discusses it in numerous works, including the account of humanity's fall in *Literal Meaning of Genesis*, bks. 9–11; Aquinas defines it as a "habit" inherited as "disposition" or "second nature" in *ST* I-II, q81.a1; Calvin affirms it in his discussion of the fall in *Institutes* 2.1.

start to do the same. In our next generation, *that* becomes the norm of how political process works, and our society is so much worse for it.

From the institution of slavery, to racial strife, social and economic oppression, to perpetuations of wars, the wrongs that are established in one generation become the *norm* for the next. Sometimes such wrongs become so established that they become invisible, with the consequence that our missed marks no longer even register in our consciousness.

We may again protest that this is unfair. Not all of what's wrong with our world now is *our fault*; we just had a terrible inheritance. Though again, we'd be selectively ignoring how most of the good things in our world now are also *not our* doing, but what our previous generations accomplished, sometimes at great cost.

And so, the voice of truth is still relentless. You've inherited good as well as bad, truth as well as errors, blessing as well as curse; none of which you worked for. So, what did you do with what you inherited? If some wrong was invisible to your generation, was there no way to notice what was wrong? And the sin you inherited, all the lost world that could have been, is there nothing you can do now to head back toward it? Is there nothing you can do to make the world you inherited better? *Not* perfect, *but better*. To turn away from the wrong direction you've been heading and take some steps, any step, toward the right direction? You may still miss the mark, but at least, you can hit closer to it. You may find yourself to be the only one who's trying to turn back. But, even if no one else is beside you, is there nothing *you can do* alone to make yourself, and your world, better? *Closer to the mark*? Closer to God, who is Love? Toward the direction that the Person of God that is speaking *beckons* to you?

Because *that's* the call to repentance.

But doing that is *costly*. There are things we'll have to do, privileges and conveniences to give up, resources to spend, people to reconcile, a past to make restitutions for, and grudges to let go or forgive. And we may say that it is unfair that *we* have to bear the cost when so many before us haven't, and so many of our peers won't, even now.

But if we don't pay the cost, the *sin remains. That's just how life is*— that's how our *reality* is structured. And *that* is "God speaking."

THE COST OF SIN IS THE "JUDGMENT"

Our lives, and our world today, in an important sense, is God's judgment upon us; it is what our speech-like reality has unfolded from everything we've done. And I mean the word "judgment" in a neutral sense here. If our world is somewhat just, fair, and beautiful, if we live among people who are kinder, more loving, more admirable, who make us love life more, then, to that extent, God has judged in our favor. And many such things are not *our* doing, but the "good" we've inherited, just as we've inherited the "bad."

Now, I need to emphasize that this is by no means saying that the rich and the prosperous are blessed by God, while the poor are punished, especially not in the increasingly globalized world we live in, where one society's wealth is often built from the deprivation of another. The direction of "better" is that of love, not wealth, after all. This is encapsulated in Jesus's teaching, "Blessed are you who are poor, for yours is the kingdom of God, but, woe to you who are rich," followed by "Blessed are those who hunger and thirst for righteousness, for they will be filled."[7]

But the general idea still stands; what we do is judged by God; the world that comes about and the kind of lives we come to lead are God's judgment upon us. And if we have strayed horribly, and each subsequent generation inherits a world and practice far worse than before, then a time will come when the weight of neglect, lies, and injustice will bring everything down around us, so that "we will perish together."

And that's why the idea of sin and judgment haunts us even now, even when we don't use those exact words anymore. Possibilities, both of a much better world and a much worse one, which reality will unfold from our own actions and character, loom before us. We hope and fear the judgment they imply. Now, this may seem like a departure from a more popular notion of the judgment of God that many of us have. But that's because there are two kinds of judgments.

Let me use an everyday example. There are very strict traffic laws against drinking and driving. The reason for this is obvious. Given how our human body works and given the laws of physics that govern the force of your moving vehicle—both of which are, again, the *Logos*, "God

---

7. Luke 6:20b, 24 and Matt 5:6, respectively. I've chosen the different Gospels to articulate this point more clearly, but the differences between the exact wording of Jesus's Beatitudes between Luke and Matt—for example, "poor," as opposed to "poor in spirit"—is the subject of many discussions in biblical studies. But I think the relevance of the core thrust of his message stands.

speaking"—if you drink and drive, there's a strong chance you'll get into an accident, which may harm or kill you or other people.

So, two kinds of judgments can befall you if you drink and drive. First is that you get into an accident and heavily injure yourself. This is the natural consequence of your action, of you missing the mark. The second is that you may be stopped by a police officer and incur a heavy legal punishment. This is not a natural consequence; it's something that's imposed on you by those who are trying to prevent the first kind of judgment from happening; it is a punishment as well as a personal warning.

Now, for Christianity, God can render *both* kinds of judgments. One is simply the catastrophic consequences of us missing the mark. The other is a seemingly unrelated phenomena, through which God is declaring that we've been heading toward the *first* kind of judgment. So, for example, seemingly random natural disasters in the Bible, like locust swarms, were sometimes seen as God's judgment in the second sense.[8] And how we can discern whether such things *are* the second kind of judgments that God is speaking to us is what the mosaic of life-stories in the Bible sketch out across the generations.

But, this second kind of "judgment" points to something profoundly personal in the idea of God as the judge. God is Reality, unfolding impersonally and impartially the consequences of our actions; yet, that Reality also speaks, as an inner voice, and in the warning signs outside, calling us back from the brink.

---

8. For example, the entire prophetic book of Joel is about how such a swarm is both this judgment and warning from God regarding the moral and spiritual failure of the people of God.

CHAPTER ELEVEN

Evil is parasitical to God speaking

TWO MILLENNIA AGO, CHRISTIANS were a persecuted people who followed their Lord, who himself was persecuted and crucified. Even now, outside the West, uncounted numbers of Christians are maligned, harassed, or killed for their beliefs. That's why it is the most *bitter* irony of history that in times and places that Christianity held power, religious persecutions, inquisitions, and wars were often perpetrated in its name. And even now, its most visible and vocal adherents are frequently associated with bigotry, ignorance, and hypocrisy.

So . . . what happened?

Part of the answer is revealed in the many examples where the same evils—persecutions, injustices, and murder—were perpetrated in the name of *other* religions, or by *non*-religious or anti-religious ideologies. In every instance, such acts were overlooked, covered up, or even justified by the claim for some greater good.

And this shouldn't come as a surprise. Because every evil, Christianity warns, is *parasitic* on the good. That's what it means for there to be evil in a world being spoken forth by God, who is good. Evil lurks in our very quest toward a better world. And if we ever listen to its whispers, it will not only pull us away from our quest, it will corrupt the *quest itself*. And this warning is, sadly, far too often forgotten.

"GOD"? WHAT'S THAT?

MIRRORING ACCUSATIONS OF WRONGS POINT US TO A DEEPER QUESTION

Those who denounce religion, on the one side, and those who denounce atheism, on the other side, can make for a strange sort of *mirror image* of each other.

One side, notably exemplified some years ago by the "New Atheist" authors, argues that religion is harmful to humanity, that its leaders are hypocritical and corrupt, and that inquisitions, wars, and mass murder were perpetrated in its name. And even now, religious extremists and nationalists across the world—from Buddhism and Hinduism to Judaism, Christianity, and Islam—plague their respective society with ignorance, bigotry, and violence.

Those who defend religion would respond that such people are not the "true" followers of their religion, or at least, they are not the right representatives. They'd then go on to point out that nearly every major modern state that has banned religion outright, or are *officially atheist*, such as the Soviet Union, the Khmer Rouge, North Korea, or Maoist China, were perpetrators of mass detention, deprivation, and murder, on a scale never before seen in history.[1]

Those who champion atheism would respond that such people aren't representative of the "true" atheism they promote, which defends freedom of thought, humanism, and other similar values.

However, this mirroring on both sides ignores the real and far more pressing question: Why is it that both sides have these so-called "wrong" kind of people, and why do such people tend to become so powerful—to set up states, to sway elections, to form mobs, and to police the thoughts and behaviors of their societies? Because in all the finger-pointing we ignore the greater problem—that there seems to be something in all of us that can make us become these kinds of people, the kind who justify such atrocities by our religious or non-religious allegiance.

Aleksandr Solzhenitsyn, a Nobel Prize laureate in Literature, who survived the Nazi invasion of his homeland and then the mass prison camps of the communist Soviets, pointed to this when he wrote:

---

1. Such arguments would draw upon the historical studies of the atrocities committed in the twentieth century under various political ideologies, including those that were explicitly secular and atheistic. For an example of such study, see Courtois et al., *Black Book of Communism*.

Evil is parasitical to God speaking

If only there were evil people somewhere insidiously committing evil deeds, and it were necessary only to separate them from the rest of us and destroy them. But the line dividing good and evil cuts through the heart of every human being. And who is willing to destroy a piece of his own heart?

During the life of any heart this line keeps changing place. . . . Confronted by the pit into which we are about to toss those who have done us harm, we halt, stricken dumb: it is after all only because of the way things worked out that they were the executioners and we weren't. . . .

From good to evil is one quaver, says the proverb.
And correspondingly, from evil to good.[2]

EVIL LIES WITHIN THE PARAMETERS OF REALITY THAT GOD IS SPEAKING

Whence comes evil?

Again, we're not asking *why* God would allow evil and suffering in this world—not quite. We're translating ideas. So, what we're asking is what "evil" *means* in relation to what we mean by "God." Specifically, we're asking, if "all of reality" *is* "God speaking," *and* "God is good," *how can there be any evil at all*? And there *is* evil; our reality includes dictators who send millions into prison camps to die of abuse, starvation, and exposure.

Well, since everything we say of God is an analogy, let's re-examine our analogies. Our entire reality is speech-like, and God is like the Speaker; reality unfolds like a story, and God is like the Author. So then, let's follow our analogy and think about a really compelling story in which its world and characters truly come to life—*like reality*.

How about *The Lord of the Rings* by J. R. R. Tolkien? So, here's a question. When Frodo musters his courage to embark on a dangerous quest to destroy the One Ring, is that Frodo's doing, or Tolkien's? And one answer is that it's both. But, a more precise answer is: It depends on "where" we are. *Inside* the story, it is Frodo who has set off on his quest. But when we "step out" of that frame and understand everything *as* a story, then it is Tolkien penning his actions.

However, in a truly good story, where its characters really seem alive, the author will not have their characters do something they otherwise

---

2. Solzhenitsyn, *Gulag Archipelago* 1.1.4, 168.

wouldn't; likewise, the author will not have their world behave in a way it otherwise wouldn't. Though the author speaks the story, once spoken, its characters and its world remain true *to themselves*. And in the case of Tolkien, this includes everyone, including the Dark Lord Sauron and all the horrific suffering he caused. What part of this whole story was Tolkien's doing? In one sense, *everything*. Yet, in another sense, it's actually *unclear*, because truly great authors are constrained by their respect toward their creation.

Think back on your life—especially the times you made a decision that was truly your own, which has shaped your life ever since. Was that you, or was that "reality"? Because, broadly speaking, what you did and what then unfolded *is* all part of reality. But it was also *you*. Everything you do is *your* doing, even as it is "God speaking." And our analogy of the author implies the following: God will not speak forth for us a life that we won't live out ourselves.

Moreover, we've also explored how the *Person* of God speaks *to us*, as a kind of better version of ourselves, beckoning us to a life that is more truthful, just, and loving. That kind of life will unfold our reality one more step *toward* the world where we can flourish together. But that's only if we hear and follow that voice of God. In a sense, it is only then that the reality God is "speaking" becomes closer to what the Person of God *wants* to speak.

This further refines our translations so far about "God." All of reality is "God speaking," but *we* "fill in the content" of what God speaks.

Here's a way to think about it. The speech-like character to reality—its principles, laws, and structures—form something like the *parameters* of how everything unfolds, rather than a single fixed trajectory. Again, these parameters *are* the *Logos*, "God speaking." But, *within* these parameters, we're free to live our own lives—and not only us, but each and every thing in Nature, following its own course.[3] Of course, some parameters present a wider range of freedom than others; the law of gravity doesn't exactly allow alternative ways spacetime can curve, whereas the principles of evolution

---

3. According to quantum physics, this indeterminacy, constrained by the parameters of laws, is found even in the smallest scale of our physical universe. And this indeterminacy in our world is also amplified by emerging complexity in Nature, such as is seen in the evolution of life, consciousness, and human society. The question of what it then means for God to create, and act upon, such Nature, characterized by this indeterminacy and complexity, has led to a robust discourse between theology and contemporary science. For examples, see Ellis, "Physics, Complexity, and the Science–Religion Debate"; Gregersen, "Emergence and Complexity"; Russell, "Quantum Physics."

open an unimaginable number of paths that life can evolve. And what we humans can do is constrained only by our imagination and physical limitations. What unfolds *within* these parameters is also "God speaking." But here, we are also *participating*, or "filling in," what is being spoken.

But, God not only speaks and unfolds our reality; God also speaks to us. In fact, not only to us. Our refined analogy suggests that at some level, God also personally "speaks *to*" each and every thing in creation, within its own respective parameters.[4] So, God not only speaks to set the parameters of Nature, God can personally "call upon" it to unfold in a particular way; this may include ways that are extraordinary and beyond our imagination, which we call "miracles."

This means that any discussion about suffering in a world that God is speaking forth will need to keep this particular analogy in mind. For example, how much freedom does Nature have in regard to something like *weather* within the parameters set by the Logos of God and by what God may specifically call it to do? That's beyond what we can explore in this book though. Here, we're concerned with moral evil, which leads us to our next point.

We explored how God personally speaks within us in the form of a better version of ourselves, beckoning us toward a world in which we can flourish. But we humans can ignore that—or mock it, denigrate it, and shout it down. This is core to the meaning of "sin" in Christianity; we "miss the mark," because we "rebel against" this Person of God. It is that very freedom we have, within the parameters that God is speaking *in regard to us*, that makes moral evil *possible*.

EVIL IS A PRIVATION, OR A DEFECT, MADE UPON WHAT IS "REAL"

So, evil is possible because we can "fill in" what God is speaking, *even as* we shut out what God is speaking *to us*. However, the irony is that we can do this only *because* God is still "speaking" everything else at a more

---

4. This idea that God both speaks the parameters of creation, *and* speaks *to it* is alluded to in passages like Jer 33:25-26 (NIV): "This is what [Yahweh] says: 'If I have not made my covenant with day and night and established the laws of heaven and earth, then I will reject the descendants of Jacob and David my servant"; or Job 38:8, 10-11 (NIV): "Who shut up the sea . . . when I fixed limits for it and set its doors and bars in place, when I said, 'This far you may come and no farther; here is where your proud waves halt'?"

fundamental level—speaking the very world in which we live, and even our own currently beating heart. "God speaking" what is *good* is the *condition and ground* of our evil.

Here's another way to think about it. We've considered how our reality is structured so that things like truthfulness, justice, and love enable us to flourish together, but deceit, injustice, and malice will lead us to perish together. However, no human society would ever *start from* pure deceit, injustice, and malice—it would tear itself apart before it got going. We need some society, with some degree of goodness, for us to then turn it into a festering arena of distrust, cruelty, and violence.

Which is to say, evil *needs* good to exist, whereas good does not need evil. In fact, if there were no evil at all, what we call "good" now would have just been, well, *plain reality*—"God speaking."

Evil is *parasitic*; and it is parasitic on "God speaking."[5]

There's actually a traditional theological formula for this in Christianity: evil is a "privation." That is to say, evil does not exist in itself, but is rather the "absence" of good.[6] An illness, in this sense, is the absence of health; moral vice is the absence of virtue.

Of course, at first glance, this view seems to be obviously wrong, since evil really exists; disease and cancer *exist*, as do things like malice, hatred, or cruelty; these aren't something ephemeral.

But, this Christian formulation is not saying that evil does not "exist" in *that* sense. Rather, it's saying that evil is a *defect in* something that exists, which would otherwise be "good." It is a twisted, distorted taint on what God is "speaking." In that sense, evil cannot exist *on its own*; it needs a host, sort of like a virus or a cancer. This is the reason for our previous formulation: evil is *parasitical*.

For one thing, evil is parasitic on existence in order for it to, well, exist. The Christian position is that "existence" as such is good. Which is *not* to say that "not existing" is evil per se. We can think about "existence" in this context as something being "*real*." So, when do we use the word "real" to mean something good? We may say, "You are being real," or "That

---

5. C. S. Lewis put it this way: "A sound theory of value demands... that good should be able to exist on its own while evil requires the good on which it is parasitic in order to continue its parasitic existence" (*God in the Dock*, 5).

6. For example, both Augustine and Aquinas regarded existence to be "good"; so, Augustine understood evil as "corruption" of what is good, and Aquinas defined evil as a defect. See Augustine, *Confessions*, 7.12, 16; Aquinas, *ST* I.q48.aa1–4, q49.a1.

idea presents something *real*." Even regarding a work of fiction, we may say, "There was something profoundly real about that story."

And this is especially the case in terms of moral good. So, for instance, feeding the hungry and making peace with our neighbors are goods, but *only if* we make them happen for *real*. Of course, intending to do something good is better than not even intending it. But if you merely intended to do something good, like feeding the hungry, but didn't actually do it, we'd consider that a moral failure, at least to some degree. When it's about doing something good, not making it happen for real makes it *less* good.

But, this isn't quite how it works with moral *evil*. Say, you intended to beat down your neighbor to take his car, yet did not make it happen for real. Now, if it was your decency or love for your neighbor that stopped you, it's not that you simply didn't make it happen. Rather, your intention itself changed, so you did something else, like asking him for a ride in his car. However, if you merely *failed* to carry out your evil intention—you flailed your fist uselessly, then tripped on your own feet—then all your moral defects are still with you; it's that you were also clumsy and weak. Your inability to make your evil plan happen for real is not some moral good; it's yet *another defect*. And if you were able to make it real—if you had the strength or the cunning to rob his car—those abilities in themselves are not what makes you evil. They merely made your evil *effective*.

Even the most murderous tyrant requires strength, leadership, and intelligence to hold his power, and such traits are *good* things; no leader would be *good* without them. Those traits simply sustain their evil desires, like how a healthy, living body will feed the cancer growing within. Evil is parasitic; it needs something good to make its effect real in the first place. But there's more to this dynamic. For evil to establish a parasitic relationship that not only makes evil possible but also makes it a part of our very character, it needs to masquerade itself *as* something good.

DIFFERENT LEVELS OF EVIL'S PARASITIC TAINT

Most people at least *pretend* to be good. And that's no wonder; completely amoral people will be rejected by the people around them. We won't trust people who we know will lie to us. We won't stand selfish people taking advantage of us. And we'll oppose psychopaths who won't hesitate to harm us if it suits them. We won't work with them, and we certainly wouldn't follow them knowingly. Because again, our reality is structured so that such people will pull us all down to perish together. We would, however, listen to them if we believed that they are morally good and will work for the sake of everyone—or, at least, for *our* sake.

Thus, in our society, evil usually needs to hide behind a *pretense* of goodness. The clearest example of this is when nations or states go to war. We even have a word for this: *pretext*. You really want to go to war because the neighboring country has a gold mine, and you want both its gold and the slaves who'll mine it. But, what you'll claim as the reason for this war will be that this country is secretly planning to use that gold to invade your country and enslave your people. And why lie? Because people are more willing to fight and die for a just cause, like fighting tyranny and defending their families, than for lining up your coffers with your neighbor's gold.

And any belief system that stands as the foundation of morality and spiritual inspiration for your people, whether it's religion or some non-religious ideology, is a very powerful and ready source of such pretexts. This means that before we point to some religious or political view as the "culprit" of some wrong, we need to first remember that such pretenders are very adaptive. In societies where a particular religion reigns supreme, they'll use pious pretexts. In societies where religion is outlawed, and an atheistic ideology is enshrined, they'll be fervently against such "harmful superstitions." So, their pretexts will be secular. After all, you can hardly use a pretext that the rest of your society won't acknowledge.

However, pretenders are simply making an outward show of goodness while inwardly they *know* very well their own true motivations. Even more insidious and powerful evil emerges when it feeds from people who manage to convince themselves that they are in the right. Because evil is now parasitic on an even larger and purer good.

This is what the Gospels are describing in the accounts of the Pharisees and the teachers of the law. Many of the prominent religious leaders in the days of Jesus were bitterly opposed to him. They claimed to be motivated by the concern for what is good—the laws that God had given them. So, they believed themselves rightfully outraged when they thought Jesus was breaking those commands. Jesus performed miracles of healing people on the Sabbath, a day when everyone was supposed to rest from their work. Worse, he befriended immoral people, like the tax-collectors, who extorted money from their fellow countrymen to gain favors from their oppressors, the Roman Empire. For such offenses, these Pharisees, in modern parlance I suppose, planned to "cancel" Jesus.[7]

Jesus rebuked them in response. They believed themselves to be standing for their moral principles, but beneath that façade were their true motivations: greed for honor, a sense of moral superiority, and sheer apathy or even contempt for the plight of those they saw as morally inferior. That was why these religious leaders stood at crowded places to pray loud and long, made a show of giving generous donations, taught strict adherence to moral codes, and mercilessly cast down any who failed them.[8]

And of course, these motivations can only be fulfilled when the system of morality that justifies you is sufficiently respected by the society in which you live. The Pharisees who opposed Jesus lived in a *Jewish* society; that's why they were able to convince others, *and themselves*, that they stood for some greater good—following God's commands, written in the Torah. Their status was their reward, and they could justify their contempt of others and their condemnation of an upstart religious teacher.

But *there is always something*. Whatever is considered good, admirable, or inspiring in a society is also a fount of self-justification, moral posturing, and gratifying one's ego. The Torah wouldn't justify you in the Soviet Union, but the Communist Manifesto would. You say you want a society where everyone is provided for, with food, income, and housing, and that's a good thing! So, you join the secret police, arresting the enemies of the revolution who stand in the way of that dream. Of course, it also happened to elevate you into the upper echelons of the party, and that eyesore of a neighbor was sent to the gulags—though he deserved it! Or, perhaps you want your people to embrace progress, and throw off the shackles of old thinking that has held them back. That's a good thing! So, with Mao's Little Red Book, you join the Red Guards of China, tearing down and burning old cultural artifacts, and punishing those who cling to the old, harmful ways. It's for the sake of your people, after all. It also just happened to win you praise from your comrades, and that old teacher who used to talk down to you was humiliated and beaten to death, but he deserved it!

There's always something. Some dream, some ideal, some vision for the good, that our darkest hidden impulses feed from, while at the same time justifying those very impulses. In the Bible Belt, the Bible may justify you for how badly you treat certain people. But if you live where the

---

7. Matt 6:2–5; 9:1–13; 12:1–14; 15:1–14.
8. Matt 23:13–28; Luke 11:42–46.

Bible won't do that, perhaps the social justice movement might, or perhaps environmental activism might. *There's always something.* Something that's respected, something that aspires for what is good, something that inspires everyone else, to give them meaning and purpose, something that seems true, at least in some important way.

And so, Solzhenitsyn, recalling the Soviet gulags, remarked:

> To do evil a human being must first of all believe that what he's doing is good. . . . Macbeth's self-justifications were feeble—and his conscience devoured him. Yes, even Iago was a little lamb, too. The imagination and spiritual strength of Shakespeare's evildoers stopped short at a dozen corpses. Because they had no *ideology*.
>
> Ideology—that is what gives evildoing its long-sought justification and gives the evildoer the necessary steadfastness and determination. That is the social theory which helps to make his acts seem good instead of bad in his own and others' eyes, so that he won't hear reproaches and curses but will receive praise and honors. That was how the agents of the Inquisition fortified their wills: by invoking Christianity; the conquerors of foreign lands, by extolling the grandeur of their Motherland; the colonizers, by civilization; the Nazis, by race; and the Jacobins (early and late), by equality, brotherhood, and the happiness of future generations.[9]

And if everything real, and everything good, is "*God speaking*," what you want is something that *sounds like* that. Because a show of following it will elevate you in the eyes of others, and of course, more importantly, *yourself*. It is the greatest cover, the most powerful masquerade, from which you can impose your darker will. Or as the apostle Paul wrote, "for Satan himself masquerades as an angel of light. It is not surprising, then, if his servants also masquerade as servants of righteousness."[10]

PARASITE'S FINAL QUESTION: WHAT DOES YOUR TRUTH ENTITLE YOU TO DO?

There's one crucial point we have not addressed so far. And it has to do with how, unlike my examples of religion, environmentalism, or whatnot, I do *not* think that the atrocities committed by communism in the twentieth century were solely due to this masquerade; I suspect that there's something

---

9. Solzhenitsyn, *Gulag Archipelago*, 1.1.4, 173–74.
10. 2 Cor 11:14–15a (NIV).

Evil is parasitical to God speaking

in this ideology *itself* that led to the horrors that unfolded in nearly every country it reigned over. Now, historians can debate whether my suspicion is true—we won't. My point here is, *if* it is true, it'd be due to *how* this ideology answers this following question: What does your truth entitle you to do?

What I mean is this. There are certain things, important things, that we believe are true. Say, the way we should live as individuals, or how we should think in order to be more rational, informed, and wise, or what we need to do to enact justice, correct inequities, and protect our planet. And so on. But, there are always people who don't believe in our truths or agree with us on what must be done. Now, is that because they are ignorant or malevolent? Perhaps. It could just be that they're just self-serving. I mean, when we're trying to make genuine changes—say, to dismantle some great injustice in our society—we can expect that, generally speaking, those who'd gain from these changes would welcome it, while those who won't be affected either way would be indifferent, and those who'd stand to lose from it would oppose it. Whichever the reason is, we have oppositions. So, what do we do? Debate? Persuade? Win an election?

Let's skip all that though. Say, we then find ourselves with power to enact our beliefs or ideals over any objection or opposition. We have the mandate. Or the needed leverage, or influence, or brute force. Yet, even then, these people still oppose us, and stubbornly stand in our way. Perhaps they were even the very people who previously suppressed *our* views in *brutal ways*. But *now*, we have power over them.

And what if we believe these people are really reprehensible and responsible for a lot of harm? Maybe we think their influence needs to be "curtailed" a bit—for the sake of everyone else, of course. Some actions against them are necessary, or justified, or at least—what's the word?—"understandable." Perhaps we can "re-educate" them; what if that doesn't work? Maybe they'd need to be put away, away from where they'll cause harm—to others, to themselves, to our *cause*.

So, what does our truth entitle us to do, when *we have the power*?

How we answer this question is the final test, the final temptation. Even if we do genuinely want what's true and good; even if there's no masquerade, neither pretense nor hypocrisy, there's one more vector for parasitic evil to infect us. And since we've drawn on *The Lord of the Rings* for our analogies this chapter, here's one scene from it:

> "You are wise and powerful. Will you not take the Ring?"

"God"? What's That?

"No!" cried Gandalf, springing to his feet. "With that power I should have power too great and terrible. And over me the Ring would gain a power still greater and more deadly." His eyes flashed and his face was lit as by a fire within. "Do not tempt me! For I do not wish to become like the Dark Lord himself. Yet the way of the Ring to my heart is by pity, pity for weakness and the desire of strength to do good. Do not tempt me! I dare not take it, not even to keep it safe, unused. The wish to wield it would be too great for my strength."[11]

Frodo offers the wizard Gandalf—who in Tolkien's Middle-Earth Legendarium is a servant of *Eru-Iluvatar*, God and Creator—the One Ring that grants uncontested power over the mortal world. Gandalf vehemently refuses it. His answer to our question was: Even the greatest of our truths and purposes *never* entitles us to use power that compels others to fulfill it. Such an act inevitably corrupts it, *and* us. The call to use that power is the final snare of the voice of parasitic evil.

And, according to the Christian Gospels, that voice spoke to Jesus, before he began his ministry to speak to humanity what God is speaking.

---

11. Tolkien, *Fellowship of the Ring*, 81.

CHAPTER TWELVE

Why God still speaks

Every truth is hearing God speaking. I suppose this means that what we're reaching toward, fumbling, tumbling, yet inching forward, by translating the ideas of "God," is also *that*—trying to hear God speak, where we are, then putting what we hear into words. Yet, some truths cannot merely be explored and exposited. Some must be sung; some shouted with awe. Others must be howled; they must be wailed in anguish.

All of reality is "God speaking," yet we "fill in" *our* portion of what God is speaking. But what if we've been covering our ears from the Person of God speaking to us? What if we've faced that Person, in the form of a better version of who we could be, beckoning us to relate to reality more meaningfully, truthfully—just one step more—but we've turned and stepped the other way? Because it was too hard, or it offended our pride? What if in doing so, evil has defaced how we've filled in the content of God speaking? And what if this rots the very world God is speaking, even now? Just *how* should such truths be spoken? And what if we, having shouted down that voice of God, turn and strike each other, while declaring that *this* is what God is speaking?

If every truth is hearing God speaking, what would we "hear"?
Because some truths must be wailed; they must be wept aloud.
And so I shall, here.

"GOD"? WHAT'S THAT?

HINDSIGHT IS 20/20, BUT FORESIGHT IS NOT BLIND

We wail at the tragedies of our human history, at the horrors we could've avoided. We say, "if only"—if we'd known this; if we'd done that. For hindsight is 20/20. Those of us in the present can clearly see the obvious past mistakes, bad decisions, and moral failings, far better than those who lived back then could. If only—if only we knew then what we know now!

But, were there *really* no signs back then that we were headed in the wrong direction? Was there really no way for us to have chosen differently, chosen a better path? Were our mistakes inevitable? Perhaps sometimes, yes, but *every* time? Hindsight may be 20/20, but foresight is not blind! We could see *something*.

When we were struggling with the global COVID-19 pandemic, did we not see it coming before? People were warning us for years to prepare for such a pandemic; we even had blockbuster movies and games that were basically all about that. So, why were we caught so unprepared? And what about the current environmental and climate catastrophes, political and social polarization, racial strife, or threats to free speech? For every ill that we face today, we're confronted with a question from the voice that speaks our most truthful thoughts. Did we really not notice?

Because that's how it *always* is.

Was there no way for the Germans living in the 1930s to at least fear that following the fiery and flattering words of this charismatic, ultra-nationalistic, rising political star would lead to a dark future? Now, they may not have known that it would lead to the systematic murder of millions and the devastation of the world, including their homes. But were there no people who spoke up? Was there no voice in their hearts telling them that there was a *scent of blood* in that man's words?

Was there no way for anyone to notice that the communist movement that swept across the world, promising a new age of secular, material paradise, subtly harbored a kind of arrogant callousness, if not malevolence—the kind that Solzhenitsyn would later witness in the Gulag Archipelago?[1] They may not have known that it would bring forth regimes so tyrannical that uncounted millions would disappear in the resulting famines, correction camps, and purges. But, was there no one who noticed a coldness in

---

1. For just the early selection of vivid examples, see Solzhenitsyn, *Gulag Archipelago*, 1.1.1, 11; 1.1.2, 37–38; 1.1.3; 2.3.5, 147–49.

the air, a falseness in those who stood at the forefront, that reminded them of, yes, the *religious hypocrites* of the past they so despised?

Was there no reason, nor voice of conscience that spoke centuries ago against exploiting and enslaving millions of Indigenous peoples, or abducting and transporting millions of Africans as slaves, all for profit? Perhaps modern ideas like the rights of all peoples may have been only dimly perceived back then, but was there no one among them who said, *"This is crossing the line"*? Indeed, weren't there some dissenting voices—in the churches and missions, in the colonies, in their society?[2] And if nothing else, from the agonized cries of justice among the Indigenous and the Africans themselves?

And there *were* voices, perhaps from someone else, perhaps from within: a voice that *spoke the truth*, which always points to the Person of "God speaking" for that generation. The truth humanity can hear may be limited by the moral and cultural level of when and where they live. But there is always *something*, some level of truth they still could've known, some level of moral clarity they still should've reached, even then. How else could there have been voices that spoke against their wrongs?

So, why did they not listen? Why do *we* not listen?

For this question is posed even to our individual lives. When we turn to look at ourselves today, at what we have become, if we are horrified by what we see, did we really never know, not even a bit, that this was what we were becoming? If we found our family bonds broken, love we held now turned bitter—or perhaps never held at all—did we really never know, or at least fear, that this was where we were headed? If we *crossed* a line we never should've crossed, said words or did things that ruined our work, our relationships, or our innermost lives; if we fell into addiction, or gambling, or into a vicious cycle of hatred; was there really nothing that spoke to us back then, no voice within us, that stopped us? Something that *screamed* at us as we stepped across that line? And if something did speak to us, a voice—a voice that spoke the truth, which is the Person of *God speaking*—to turn back, to follow another path, *why didn't we listen*?

---

2. For example, in 1542, Bartolomé de Las Casas, a Catholic missionary, wrote about the atrocities against the Indigenous peoples in the colonial Americas and demanded radical reform, despite threats to his life. See Las Casas, *Short Account of the Destruction of the Indies*. Ironically, Las Casas himself at first supported importing African slaves to alleviate the Indigenous suffering, only to vehemently regret and retract it later in his life. Then, in 1688, a group of Quakers in Pennsylvania lodged a formal petition of protest against African slavery. See Carey, *From Peace to Freedom*, 70–104.

"GOD"? WHAT'S THAT?

Or more importantly: What happened to that voice so that things turned out the way they did? What did we do to that voice?

THE COST OF WHAT WE'VE DONE TO THE VOICE OF GOD

We actually do know what happened with those voices, at least, when those voices are from the outside—from other people. Because when we have the power to silence them, we do; when who don't, we simply ignore them.

There's a long line of such figures in our history. Nelson Mandela was imprisoned for twenty-seven years for speaking out against the Apartheid regime in South Africa. But he was fortunate, since he saw the regime fall, and then became the president. Others were less fortunate. Mahatma Gandhi, after a lifetime of imprisonment and struggle, saw his country's independence, only to be murdered by a *fellow* Hindu for speaking out against religious violence. Rev. Martin Luther King Jr. never saw the dreams of racial equality come to fruition in his lifetime before he was murdered on April 4, 1968. But even they were fortunate because they saw their movements in motion.

There must have been other people—people we don't even know about—who were silenced before anyone heard them. There must have been such people, who had quietly, perhaps with courage and conviction, or perhaps with fear and trembling, stood up for truth, justice, goodness; who testified against what was wrong.

Or perhaps, they didn't even need to say anything. Centuries before Martin Luther King, before even the very first abolitionist protest, there would have been, perhaps, a young child from Africa, looking with innocence at her potential slaver. And her very gaze alone would have been to the slaver, well, the voice of God that *speaks every truth*, speaking without words, but speaking nonetheless, the truth that *this* is a real person who he's about to consign to a lifetime of suffering and servitude. How many times did that slaver silence that voice?

What did he do to silence it? Perhaps he silenced it so many times it no longer spoke. He may even have justified himself by some verses in the Bible—a time-honored strategy favored by the devil himself, according to the Christian Gospels, when he quoted the Bible to tempt none other than Jesus.[3] After all, evil is parasitic, and its greatest power lies in its mas-

---

3. Matt 4:6; Luke 4:9–11.

querade. Perhaps, the slaver didn't even need to do any of that, because the previous generation of slavers had already done all that for him. Because in this way, sin is inherited. The wrongs of the past become the norm of the present.

So, how many of those voices have been silenced? Voices that speak the truth, bear witness to what is good. How many are being silenced today? Those whose names we will never know. Many voices of conscience. Many voices of truth. Even now, across the world. Every day. Every second. Tick tock. Tick tock.

Is that what God was saying in that story in the Bible when Cain murdered his brother Abel—when God declares to him and now to us, "The earth itself, which received the spilled blood of those you murdered, cries out to me against you"?[4]

And there's a *cost* to that. Because the first kind of God's judgment is that God *will* speak the reality we've filled in—the world we've ruined—and *there* we will live, we and our children.

Still, every truth is hearing *God speaking*. And so, the voice of truth, the Person of Reality that speaks to us, will exhort us to pay heed to the kind of hell we are making now.

And there's a cost every time we ignore or silence that voice, and the consequences will become larger and larger. Until one day, the cost will come due, to be paid *in full*. Lives of millions; lands and countries devastated; the cries of the victims eventually joined by the cries of those who were once perpetrators.

So it was that when the American Civil War devastated his nation, Abraham Lincoln prayed and hoped for its end, but feared that this cost was now due. As the war spilled the blood of countless white men and tears of white women, as if to balance the blood and tears of black men and women shed before, he asked why God would not grant those who were finally fighting to free the slaves an easy victory. And he came to the sobering conclusion that God was demanding the account of the centuries of slavery, both from those who enslaved them, and from those who, until this war, had been complicit.[5]

---

4. Gen 4:10–11; Matt 23:34–35; Luke 11:50–51.

5. Lincoln would voice this conclusion with the following words: "Fondly do we hope—fervently do we pray—that this mighty scourge of war may speedily pass away. Yet, if God wills that it continue, until all the wealth piled by the bondsman's two hundred and fifty years of unrequited toil shall be sunk, and until every drop of blood drawn with the lash shall be paid by another drawn with the sword, as was said three thousand

"GOD"? WHAT'S THAT?

Or to translate for our Godless world, the *cost* becomes larger as the sin becomes more entrenched. If the first slaver had stopped his hand, as he gazed into the eyes of another human being he was about to enslave, if he had *heard God speak* in that gaze—if he had not ignored or dismissed the voice and heard it—the cost would have been different. To say the least. The more entrenched slavery became, the stronger the force to defend slavery became, each passing day, year, and century. For more and more people profited from the labor of the enslaved, justified it, looked the other way, and ignored every voice of God speaking. And one day, it was so strong that nothing less than a protracted, all out, bloody war that would ravage the entire nation would dislodge it.

That's how reality unfolds—and that *how* is "God speaking."

And Reality—God—demands a cost for the world we make.

Hindsight is 20/20, yes, but our foresight is not blind. Given our limitations, of our culture, our moral norms, our understanding, could we still have made our lives, our world, better than it is *now*, more loving, more just, more truthful? If yes, then *why didn't we*?

The *why* is our sin, and its answer is: Because we silenced the voice that informed us we were missing the mark. Perhaps the voice from within us. Perhaps from someone else. The voice that turned out to have spoken the truth. And in doing so, we've silenced the Person of God that speaks to us. Perhaps unknowingly. Or, perhaps we justified silencing it, sometimes with our ideology, and sometimes with supreme irony, by appealing to God. But we should have known what we were doing. Or at the very least, should have feared what we may be committing.

HOW SHOULD GOD SPEAK TO A WORLD THAT SILENCES GOD'S EVERY VOICE?

Christians believe that Jesus Christ is God speaking, who became a human being. The entire Christian Bible maps God speaking to us, by sketching our millennia-long journey to this person; the mosaic of life-stories of the people in it, piece by piece, depicts the character of the Person of God that spoke with them, which again points to this person. Jesus is God speaking

---

years ago, 'the judgments of the Lord are true and righteous altogether'—so still it must be said 'the judgments of the Lord are true and righteous altogether'" ("Second Inaugural Address").

in our midst, teaching, inspiring, and exhorting us ever toward the horizon where the Person of God forever beckons. How *he* speaks is how *He* speaks.[6]

But, human history is the history of silencing the voices of God.

And this includes those who claim allegiance to God, the religious leaders and teachers in the Bible who decried their ancestors by saying, "If only we lived back then, we'd never have shed the blood of those who spoke what God is speaking to us."

But, Jesus responds, "Your ancestors killed them, and you decorate their tombs. Doing so, you complete what they started. And God is saying, 'I'm sending you prophets and sages and teachers. Some you will kill, others you will torture, the rest you will drive away.' And the cost for all of it will be demanded of you."[7]

Yet, then how *should God*—how should *he*—speak to a world that will silence him? According to the Gospels, that was the question Jesus was confronted with before he began to teach. After forty days in the desert, hungry from his fasting yet at the height of his spiritual awareness, the devil—the voice of the parasitic evil—speaks to him.

"If you are the Son of God, turn these stones into bread."

"If you are the Son of God, perform a miracle by jumping off the temple, because God promised to protect you."

"I will give you all the powers of the kingdoms of this world, if you would just bow to me."[8]

And Jesus rejects what the devil speaks, by drawing upon what God has spoken to the people through the generations—the Scriptures. We can understand these temptations in a more general way, as testing his faith in God regarding the things he'd need in life. But, this confrontation points to something more. Jesus was about to begin his ministry, to speak what God is speaking to the world. And the devil did not merely say, "Aren't you hungry? Turn stones into bread," or, "If you have faith in God, ask for miracles."

Instead, it said, "*If you are the Son of God.*" That is, if Jesus really is the *Person* of God speaking to us, if he really is the version of ourselves we will forever journey toward, if he is the voice we've been silencing, *then*, the devil declares, this is what he should—what *God should*—do to save humanity: Use power!

---

6. "Jesus answered: 'Don't you know me, Philip, even after I have been among you such a long time? Anyone who has seen me has seen the Father'" (John 14:9a NIV).

7. Matt 23:29–39; Luke 11:47–51.

8. Matt 4:1–11; Luke 4:1–13.

"God"? What's That?

"Use power for that. Use power to fill their hunger, so they'll be compelled to follow you. Use your power to perform miracles, and make them submit. Or else, take for yourself the power that the empires of this world, which rule over them, possess."[9]

But not only does Jesus reject these temptations, his subsequent life and ministry, recounted in the Gospels, explicitly presents a counterpoint to each of them.

Jesus *does* bring forth bread. Out of a single packed meal, he brings forth enough food to feed several thousand. *But* when people try to declare him the king in response, he immediately leaves them. He *can* bring forth bread, but *that* will not be what makes him the "Son of God."

Jesus performs miracles. He healed the sick and even raised the dead. Yet often, he tells people to keep this a secret *until* he dies on the cross. He has power to perform miracles, but he will not use it to make people submit to him as the "Son of God."

Neither the bread nor the miracles were to be tools of power. And it's a very specific kind of power—power to compel others, to use it as *currency* to buy and sell "truth," to buy and sell "love." Yet, this currency is such that it will eventually devour what it buys and sells until only it remains. For evil is parasitical and kills its host, then shrivels away by itself until it infects its next host.

The Person of God that speaks to us simply beckons us toward truth and toward love. Perhaps that is why our speech-like reality is such that *we* can fill in what God speaks. Perhaps, the reality that God is speaking is also an invitation to participation, freely offered, at profound cost. Perhaps that is yet another analogy of God—for Reality—one we can't quite comprehend nor imagine yet.

And Jesus rejects everything that will let parasitic evil devour what God beckons us to: love and truth that will sustain our proper, ongoing relationship with Reality. So, *his* power, God's power, will *not be currency*; it will be given freely, without condition, as God responding to suffering.

But *others*, including those who claim to follow God, trade in that currency. And they *crucify* those without it.

---

9. This confrontation is what is so powerfully portrayed in "The Grand Inquisitor," a story told by an atheist character in *The Brothers Karamazov* by Fyodor Dostoyevsky. In the story, the Grand Inquisitor arrests Jesus who has returned to earth and declares that he should have done what the devil said, i.e., to use power to compel humanity, for their own sake.

So, on the day Jesus was finally crucified, Pilate asked Jesus, "Are you a king?" And Jesus replied, "My kingdom is not a kingdom of this world. Or else, my disciples would be fighting for me. I'm a king, and my kingdom is Truth."

Because *that* is—that *always is*—God speaking to us.

"What is truth?" Pilate asked him then. What is truth without the currency of power?

But what is truth, when it's sold and bought with that currency?

So, the religious leaders of his day, together with the secular—or their equivalent to secular—rulers, tortured him, publicly humiliated him, and then nailed him to a cross to die. Mobs of people joined in, to sneer at his powerlessness. Others turned away, feeling that this was business as usual—nothing that hasn't happened before. Those who followed him abandoned him in terror and dismay.

That's the Christian account of the crucifixion of Jesus, when humanity, once more and with finality, silenced the voice of God.[10]

Those who hoped to see God through this man, Jesus, fled and hid. And despaired. Yes . . . we despaired. Because it seems God will always be silenced. And in our worst moments, even we sneer at God's powerlessness, and say, "Well, there's nothing to it, after all."

But, where does that leave us? A powerless voice of God, who is always silenced?

I suppose we still get snippets of that voice here and there before we silence it, so that humanity will stumble along in its history and attain *some* good and some truths along the way—because we do make some progress, though nearly every time with suffering, agony, and blood.

Or, perhaps those who seek the voice of God must always make a deal with the devil, to shake the hands Jesus had refused, so that *we too* are not crucified. That means, of course, our hearing of the voice of God speaking will eventually become distorted, until the hallowed halls where God speaks to us in one generation become in the next the dark palaces that echo with intrigue, religious hypocrisy, and tyranny. But, *that's* the best we can hope for. Because after all, Jesus died. And the high priests and kings who killed him still reigned.

---

10. The Gospel accounts of the suffering and crucifixion of Jesus are found in Matt 27:27–50; Mark 15:9–37; Luke 23:8–46; John 19:1–37.

"GOD"? WHAT'S THAT?

WHY GOD STILL SPEAKS

Every Easter, churches across the world gather together and declare the words, "Christ is risen."

And Christians throughout the world respond, "He is risen indeed."

When Jesus died on the cross, a few sympathizers of Jesus, those who belonged among the powerful but still longed to hear God speak and see the true reign of God, approached those who had killed Jesus. At least let us bury him, one said—we'll provide the grave and the burial costs.

Go ahead, said the one who killed him; we've no more business with a corpse. And so, Jesus was buried in a grave.

Then, on Sunday morning, some women who had been Jesus's followers went to his grave, to mourn and to treat the dead body of God speaking to humanity. There, they would accept that *this* was the way of our world, our destiny, our *perpetual sin*.

They arrived only to find his grave broken open, the rock that sealed him in rolled to the side. In the empty tomb, they received a message.

"You're looking for a dead body. But, he is risen! So, go, and tell the ones who are in despair."

You saw the voice of God silenced.

But *God still speaks*.[11]

And some truths that are to be spoken, must be sung.

So, the Christian message sings of God speaking all that ever is; it sings of the Person of God that speaks, who became one of us. And it sings how he speaks even now.

And though sometimes we may want God to speak in vengeance and retribution to those who silenced him, God does not. Because we *all* take part in silencing the voice of God. That's why our world is not where it could have been and should have been. That's why our lives are not what they could be and should be.

Yet, *God still speaks*.

And his words do not hold condemnation for any of us who have silenced him. His voice is not tinged with even an echo of that contempt that our own voices drip with, when speaking of our many failings as a species. Because his is the voice of the Speaker that speaks our reality, yet invites us to fill in what is being spoken, even when we continue to deface it with

---

11. The Gospel accounts of the burial of Jesus and his resurrection are recounted in Matt 27:51—28:10; Mark 15:38—16:8; Luke 23:47—24:49; John 19:38—20:29.

parasitic evil. Nor is the call of God muted with that despair or hopelessness we hold toward ourselves. Because his is the call of the Person that forever beckons us, even at our worst, and treasures a single true step even after a hundred false ones.

The voice of God speaks kindly, yet relentlessly. Once again beckoning to us. Reshaping us. Transforming us. Until everything speaks as the Person of God speaks.

And so, God *still speaks*.

Even when we won't hear.

Because you cannot keep the voice of God in the grave.

"Jesus is risen," so "God still speaks."

And on this impossible witness Christianity began.

Epilogue

At the crossing of our worldviews

WE'VE NOW ARRIVED AT the border. This crossing between a Godless world and the world of Christianity is where our exploration so far has taken us, a place where we can hear its distant sounds and breathe in its faint scents. It may surprise some of us to find that we have not yet properly *crossed the border*. But our only incursion so far into that Christian world—and it was but a step in and back—was our brief "singing" in our prior chapter about the resurrection of Jesus Christ. And if that seemed like a sudden change of scenery, so to speak, it's because we haven't properly journeyed there. It was more a distant glimpse of something deep inside that world, seen from our crossing.

Here, a voice addresses me. It's not quite the voice that orients me—as far as I can be—to all of reality: the most true, the most just, the most good. But, but it's a voice I should consider. I don't know if it would've been considered *a* god in ancient times. Anyway, it asks: "Is what we've explored so far really the Christian understanding of God?"

Well, not quite, and not *yet*. Because we've only just arrived at the border. We've been translating the idea of "God" for those of us who live in a Godless world. But when translating from one vastly different language—or in this case, worldview—to another, we work with the constraints of these languages. Yet, as we translate more and more vocabulary, the previous translations can take on greater meaning. That's what I hope has happened as we explored more and more translations on "God" throughout this book.

And our translations should have enabled us to perceive another world, perhaps even be persuaded by it. That's what it means to have reached the border. We no longer inhabit only our old world, but can somehow perceive a different one—another world now juxtaposed over the previous one. Yet, here's where our analogy of a journey reaches its own limits. Because in this strange familiar land, it's not that we have moved, but that the lands around us have been re-introducing themselves to us. Here, God is not an alien. This very world and its horizons is "God speaking," the sound the ground on which we stand, the tone the skies splashed with vibrant colors.

And from here, at this "crossing," we'll be able to explore the layout of this new world, so strange yet familiar. That layout is the world sung by Genesis in the Bible. Can you sense its wind from here? Or the stirrings of its storms? But for now, here's where we must part.

For this book is something that presents you with only the premise. If Christianity recounts a millennia-long story of how we've formed an ongoing, personal relationship with God, what we explored is the premise of *what this story is about*. Or rather, I've *translated* this premise for our Godless world. And a premise is not even a synopsis. It preps us *for* what we are to explore.

And there *is* much to explore, for we part with many unanswered questions that surround this world of Christianity and its idea of God: regarding a deeper understanding of Reality, creation, or of good and evil; about the divine inspiration of the Bible, salvation and judgment, or heaven and hell; concerns about other faiths and worldviews. And each of those would require further "translations."

However, there is something distinctive about what a Christian translator would understand as her goal—a distinctive *emphasis*, so to speak. To illustrate this point, let's compare the Christian idea of "God's speech" to that of another religion—its colleague, rival, and relative—Islam. Both, very generally speaking, would understand the cosmos as created by God's speech.[1] Yet, this "speech of God" is spoken personally *to* humanity through distinctively different means.

In Islam, there's this idea of the "Heavenly Qur'an." This is the idea that "*Kalam-Allah*"—the "actual *speech*" of God—which most Muslims believe is "eternal and uncreated," was then spoken to humanity in Arabic as their holy book, the Qur'an. And this idea of the "Heavenly Qur'an" seems to parallel the Christian idea of the *Logos*, as "God speaking."[2]

---

1. Qur'an 2.117, trans. M. A. S. Abdel Haleem, "Originator of the heavens and the earth. When He decrees a matter, He only says to it, 'Be,' and it is."

2. For references to the "Heavenly Qur'an," see for example, Qur'an 56.77–80, 85.22. For a concise overview of this idea, see Morgan, *Essential Islam*, 30–31; Morgan also remarks on the parallel between the ideas of the "Heavenly Qur'an" and the *Logos* in her discussions.

Epilogue

Yet, here's where they diverge in a crucial way, especially for our understanding of "translating" God. In Islam, "God's speech" is spoken to humanity *as a fixed text*, whereas in Christianity "God speaking" became a *human person*. Thus, their respective holy books have different functions. For Muslims, "God's speech" is the text of the Qur'an, recited into the human language of Arabic, and their prophets are its messengers, its "carriers." But for Christians, "God speaking" is a person, Jesus Christ, who lived *as* an Aramaic-speaking Jew, and the Bible is the "messenger" that "carries" his life to us.

And so, in Islam, only the *Arabic* Qur'an is really "God's speech"; translations of the Qur'an can only remain translations. This is because *God* spoke the Qur'an to humanity *in* Arabic.[3] In Christianity though, the Bible *can* be translated from its original Hebrew and Greek into different languages, yet remain "God's Word"; our English Bible is not merely a translation of the "true" Bible; it *is* the Bible—though greater authority is of course given to the original texts. This is because Christianity teaches that the Bible is meant to "point" to the One who *truly is* "God speaking" at a particular point in history. And that is the person of Jesus. Who he is and what he did is *uniquely divine*, and can never be replicated at any different time or place. He can only be "translated."

But then, here's a question: What does it mean to translate a *life*?

And the answer, if we think about it, is surprisingly simple. A translation of a text is a text; a translation of a person is a person. The person and character of that Jewish teacher in first-century Palestine who saved the world can be translated into an English-speaking person in twenty-first-century North America, going about her daily business. Such translation is *not* Jesus himself—it's a *translation*.

And these translations will mostly be partial, and often, terrible ones at that. But translate we must, for Christianity calls those partial translations "Christians," and the compilation of those translations the "church." And so, for Christians, *to live* is *to translate Christ*. The person that speaks to us as a better version of ourselves, who relate to reality more truthfully, meaningfully, and lovingly; the person that is speaking to us what the Person of God is speaking, yet accommodated for our time and place; Christians confess that this person is Jesus Christ. And to head toward that person, beckoning from that ever-moving horizon of Reality, is to translate that person into versions unique to each of us. As we do so, we'll also come

---

3. Qur'an 43.3–4; also see Morgan, *Essential Islam*, 19–22.

to embody "God speaking" more, and come to know more deeply God who indeed knows and loves us.

And the Christian Bible is the map that guides this translation. Just as the millennia-long journey it maps points to the person of Jesus, it also maps how each person and community today is to point back to Jesus by translating his life for *our* generation. Just as its mosaic of life-stories forms the portrait of the Person of God in Jesus, the Bible guides how *we* are to form that mosaic today. This is what it means when the Bible describes itself as "able to make you wise for salvation through faith in Christ Jesus," and as "God-breathed and... useful for teaching, rebuking, correcting and training in righteousness, so that the servant of God may be thoroughly equipped for every good work."[4]

So too, this book.

Our translations so far about the idea of "God" are also a guide. They point to how, from our "God*less*" world, we may understand what it'd be like to translate "God," not just in terms of ideas, but also in terms of relating to all of reality—in terms of *living a life*.

A translation guide on "God" for our Godless world.

---

4. 2 Tim 3:15b–17 (NIV).

Bibliography

Aertsen, Jan. *Medieval Philosphy and the Transcendentals: The Case of Thomas Aquinas.* Leiden: Brill, 1996.
Aquinas, Thomas. *Summa Theologiae.* Translated by the Fathers of the English Dominican Province. New York: Benziger Brothers, 1947.
Arendt, Hannah. *The Origins of Totalitarianism.* 1951. Reprint, San Diego: Harcourt Brace Jovanovich, Harvest, 1968.
Athenagoras. "A Plea for the Christians." https://www.newadvent.org/fathers/0205.htm.
Augustine. *Confessions.* Translated by Henry Chadwick. Oxford: Oxford University Press, 1991.
———. *The Literal Meaning of Genesis.* Translated by John Hammond Taylor. New York: Newman, 1982.
———. *On Christian Doctrine.* Translated by J. F. Shaw. New York: Dover, 2009.
———. *On the Trinity.* Edited by Gareth B. Matthews. Translated by Stephen McKenna. Cambridge: Cambridge University Press, 2002.
Best, Steven, and Douglas Kellner. *Postmodern Theory: Critical Interrogations.* New York: Guilford, 1991.
Bostrom, Nick. "Are You Living in a Computer Simulation?" *Philosophical Quarterly* 53.211 (2003) 243–55.
Brooke, John Hedley. *Science and Religion: Some Historical Perspectives.* Cambridge: Cambridge University Press, 1991.
Buber, Martin. *I and Thou.* Translated by Walter Kaufmann. New York: Scribner, 1970.
Buckley, Michael J. *Denying and Disclosing God.* New Haven: Yale University Press, 2004.
Burkeman, Oliver. "The One Theology Book All Atheists Really Should Read." *Guardian*, January 14, 2014.
Calvin, John. *Institutes of the Christian Religion.* Edited by John T. McNeill. Translated by Ford Lewis Battles. Philadelphia: Westminster, 1960.
Carey, Brycchan, *From Peace to Freedom: Quaker Rhetoric and the Birth of American Antislavery, 1657–1761.* New Haven: Yale University Press, 2012.
Chung, Paul Seungoh. *God at the Crossroads of Worldviews: Toward a Different Debate About the Existence of God.* Notre Dame: University of Notre Dame Press, 2016.
Clayton, Philip, ed. *The Oxford Handbook of Religion and Science.* Oxford: Oxford University Press, 2008.
Collins, Francis S. *The Language of God: A Scientist Presents Evidence for Belief.* New York: Free, 2006.

Bibliography

Courtois, Stéphane, et al. *The Black Book of Communism: Crimes, Terror, Repression.* Translated by Jonathan Murphy and Mark Kramer. Cambridge: Harvard University Press, 1999.

Curvelo, Alexandra, and Angelo Cattaneo, eds. *Interactions Between Rivals: The Christian Mission and Buddhist Sects in Japan (c.1549–c.1647).* Berlin: Peter Lang, 2022.

Dawkins, Richard. *The Selfish Gene.* 2nd ed. Oxford: Oxford University Press, 1989.

Day, John. *Yahweh and the Gods and Goddesses of Canaan.* Sheffield: Sheffield Academic, 2000.

Dostoevsky, Fyodor. *The Brothers Karamazov.* Translated by Richard Pevear and Larissa Volokhonsky. New York: Vintage, 1991.

Drews, Carl, and Weiqing Han. "Dynamics of Wind Setdown at Suez and the Eastern Nile Delta." *PLoS ONE* 5.8 (2010) e12481. https://doi.org/10.1371/journal.pone.0012481.

Durkheim, Émile. *The Elementary Forms of Religious Life.* Translated by Karen E. Fields. New York: Free, 1995.

Einstein, Albert. "On Scientific Truth." In *Ideas and Opinions*, 261–62. New York: Crown, 1954.

Eliade, Mircea. *A History of Religious Ideas.* Vols. 1–2. Translated by Willard R. Trask. Chicago: University of Chicago Press, 1978–81.

Elisonas, Jurgis. "Christianity and the Daimyo." In *The Cambridge History of Japan*, edited by John Whitney Hall and James L. McClain, 4:301–73. Cambridge: Cambridge University Press, 1991.

Ellis, George F. R. "Physics, Complexity, and the Science-Religion Debate." In *The Oxford Handbook of Religion and Science*, edited by Philip Clayton, 751–66. Oxford: Oxford University Press, 2008.

Feuerbach, Ludwig. *The Essence of Christianity.* Translated by George Eliot. New York: Dover, 2008.

Flew, Antony. "The Presumption of Atheism." In *God, Freedom, and Immortality*, 13–30. Buffalo: Prometheus, 1984.

Frei, Hans W. *The Eclipse of Biblical Narrative: A Study in Eighteenth and Nineteenth-Century Hermeneutics.* New Haven: Yale University Press, 1974.

Freud, Sigmund. *The Future of an Illusion.* Translated and edited by James Strachey. New York: Norton, 1961.

Gregersen, Niels Henrik. "Emergence and Complexity." In *The Oxford Handbook of Religion and Science*, edited by Philip Clayton, 767–83. Oxford: Oxford University Press, 2008.

Hanby, Michael. *No God, No Science? Theology, Cosmology, Biology.* Malden, MA: Blackwell, 2013.

Hart, David Bentley. *The Doors of the Sea: Where Was God in the Tsunami?* Grand Rapids: Eerdmans, 2005.

———. *The Experience of God: Being, Consciousness, Bliss.* New Haven: Yale University Press, 2013.

Hawking, Stephen. *A Brief History of Time: Updated and Expanded Edition.* 1988. Reprint, New York: Bantam, 2017.

Hawking, Stephen, and Leonard Mlodinow. *The Grand Design.* New York: Bantam, 2010.

Hendel, Ronald. "The Dream of a Perfect Text: Textual Criticism and Biblical Inerrancy in Early Modern Europe." In *Sibyls, Scriptures, and Scrolls: John Collins at Seventy*, edited by J. J. Collins, 517–41. Leiden: Brill, 2017.

Bibliography

Homer. *The Iliad.* Translated by Robert Fagles. Introduction and Notes by Bernard Knox. London: Penguin Classics, 1998.

Kuhn, Thomas S. *The Structure of Scientific Revolutions.* 3rd ed. Chicago: University of Chicago Press, 1996.

Küng, Hans. *Christianity and the World Religions: Paths to Dialogue with Islam, Hinduism, and Buddhism.* Translated by Peter Heinegg. Maryknoll, NY: Orbis, 1986.

———. *Does God Exist? An Answer for Today.* Translated by Edward Quinn. New York: Doubleday, 1980.

Isaacson, Walter. *Einstein: His Life and Universe.* New York: Simon & Schuster, 2017.

James, William. *The Varieties of Religious Experience.* Reprint, London: Penguin Classics, 1982.

Jung, Carl G. *Aion: Researches into the Phenomenology of the Self.* Translated by R. F. C. Hull. 2nd ed. Collected Works of C. G. Jung 9.2. London: Routledge, 1991.

———. *The Archetypes and the Collective Unconscious.* Translated by R. F. C. Hull. 2nd ed. Collected Works of C. G. Jung 9.1. London: Routledge, 1991.

Lakoff, George, and Mark Johnson. *Metaphors We Live By.* Chicago: University of Chicago Press, 1980.

Las Casas, Bartolomé de. *A Short Account of the Destruction of the Indies.* Translated by Nigel Griffin. London: Penguin, 1992.

Lau, D. C., trans. *Confucius: The Analects (Lun Yü).* Harmondsworth: Penguin, 1979. (Reprinted with Chinese text. Hong Kong: Chinese University Press, 1979).

———, trans. *Tao Te Ching.* London: Penguin, 1963.

Lewis, C. S. *God in the Dock: Essays on Theology and Ethics.* 1970. Reprint, Grand Rapids: Eerdmans, 2014.

Lightman, Bernard, ed. *Rethinking History, Science, and Religion: An Exploration of Conflict and the Complexity Principle.* Pittsburgh: University of Pittsburgh Press, 2019.

Lincoln, Abraham. "Second Inaugural Address." In *Abraham Lincoln: Speeches and Writings 1859–1865,* edited by Don E. Fehrenbacher, 686–87. New York: Library of America, 1989.

Lonergan, Bernard J. F. *Method in Theology.* New York: Herder and Herder, 1972.

MacIntyre, Alasdair. *After Virtue: A Study in Moral Theory.* 3rd ed. Notre Dame: University of Notre Dame Press, 2007.

———. *Three Rival Versions of Moral Enquiry.* Notre Dame: University of Notre Dame Press, 1991.

———. *Whose Justice? Which Rationality?* Notre Dame: University of Notre Dame Press, 1988.

Mackie, J. L. *The Miracle of Theism: Arguments for and against the Existence of God.* Oxford: Oxford University Press, 1982.

Marx, Karl. "Theses on Feuerbach." 1888. In *Marx/Engels Selected Works,* 1:13–15. Moscow: Progress, 1969.

McFague, Sallie. *Metaphorical Theology: Models of God in Religious Language.* Philadelphia: Fortress, 1982.

McGrath, Alister E. *Christian Theology: An Introduction.* 6th ed. Chichester: Wiley-Blackwell, 2016.

McIntyre, Lee. *Post-Truth.* Cambridge: MIT Press, 2018.

Morgan, Diane. *Essential Islam: A Comprehensive Guide to Belief and Practice.* Westport, CT: Praeger, 2009.

Bibliography

Murphy, Nancey, and George F. R. Ellis. *On the Moral Nature of the Universe: Theology, Cosmology, and Ethics.* Minneapolis: Fortress, 1996.

Nagasawa, Yujin. *The Problem of Evil for Atheists.* Oxford: Oxford University Press, 2024.

Naugle, D. K. *Worldview: The History of a Concept.* Grand Rapids: Eerdmans, 2002.

Otto, Rudolf. *The Idea of the Holy: An Inquiry into the Non-Rational Factor in the Idea of the Divine and Its Relation to the Rational.* Translated by John W. Harvey. Oxford: Oxford University Press, 1923.

Oxford Languages. "Word of the Year 2016." https://languages.oup.com/word-of-the-year/2016/.

Padgett, Alan G. "God and Miracle in an Age of Science." In *The Blackwell Companion to Science and Christianity*, edited by J. B. Stump and Alan G. Padgett, 533–42. Oxford: Blackwell, 2012.

Pew Research Center. "Global Religious Landscape." https://www.pewresearch.org/religion/2012/12/18/global-religious-landscape-exec/.

———. "Religious Landscape Study." https://www.pewresearch.org/religious-landscape-study/.

Plantinga, Alvin. *God, Freedom, and Evil.* Grand Rapids: Eerdmans, 1974.

Plato. *The Laws.* Translated by Trevor J. Saunders. Harmondsworth: Penguin Classics, 2005.

Polanyi, Michael. *Personal Knowledge: Towards a Post-Critical Philosophy.* Chicago: University of Chicago Press, 1958.

Pseudo-Dionysius the Areopagite. *The Mystical Theology.* In *Pseudo-Dionysius: The Complete Works*, translated by Colm Luibheid, 135–41. New York: Paulist, 1987.

Rees, Martin. *Just Six Numbers: The Deep Forces That Shape the Universe.* 1st American ed. New York: Basic, 2001.

Ricci, Matteo. *The True Meaning of the Lord of Heaven (Tianzhu Shiyi).* Translated by Douglas Lancashire and Peter Hu Kuo-chen. St. Louis: Institute of Jesuit Sources, 1985.

Ritchie, Stuart. *Science Fictions: How Fraud, Bias, Negligence, and Hype Undermine the Search for Truth.* New York: Metropolitan, 2020.

Rorty, Richard. *Philosophy and the Mirror of Nature.* Princeton: Princeton University Press, 1979.

Russell, Bertrand. "Is There a God?" In *The Collected Papers of Bertrand Russell.* Vol. 11, *Last Philosophical Testament, 1943–68*, edited by John Slater and Peter Köllner, 542–48. London: Routledge, 1997.

Russell, Robert John. "Quantum Physics and the Theology of Non-Interventionist Objective Divine Action." In *Oxford Handbook of Religion and Science*, edited by Philip Clayton, 579–95. Oxford: Oxford University Press, 2008.

Smart, Ninian. *Dimensions of the Sacred: An Anatomy of the World's Beliefs.* Berkeley: University of California Press, 1996.

Smith, Gregory A., et al. "The Decline of Christianity in the U.S. Has Slowed, May Have Leveled Off." *Pew Research Center's Religion & Public Life Project*, February 26, 2025. https://www.pewresearch.org/religion/2025/02/26/decline-of-christianity-in-the-us-has-slowed-may-have-leveled-off/.

Smith, Mark S. *The Early History of God: Yahweh and Other Deities in Ancient Israel.* 1990. Reprint, Grand Rapids: Eerdmans, 2002.

Bibliography

Solzhenitsyn, Aleksandr I. *The Gulag Archipelago, 1918–1956: An Experiment in Literary Investigation*. Translated by Thomas P. Whitney. 3 vols. New York: Harper & Row, 1974.

Stone, Robert E. II. "I Am Who I Am." In *Eerdmans Dictionary of the Bible*, edited by David Noel Freedman and Allen C. Myers, 624. Grand Rapids: Eerdmans, 2000.

Tallis, Raymond. *Logos: The Mystery of How We Make Sense of the World*. London: Agenda, 2018.

Tarnas, Richard. *The Passion of the Western Mind: Understanding the Ideas That Have Shaped Our World View*. New York: Ballantine, 1991.

Taylor, Charles. *A Secular Age*. Cambridge: Harvard University Press, 2007.

Tillich, Paul. *Systematic Theology*. 3 vols. Chicago: University of Chicago Press, 1951–63.

Tolkien, J. R. R. *The Fellowship of the Ring*. 1954. Reprint, London: HarperCollins, 1999.

Wheeler, John Archibald. "Information, Physics, Quantum: The Search for Links." In *Complexity, Entropy, and the Physics of Information*, edited by Wojciech H. Zurek, 354–68. Boston: Addison-Wesley, 1990.

Willard, Dallas. *Hearing God: Developing a Conversational Relationship with God*. Rev. and exp. ed. Downers Grove, IL: InterVarsity, 1999.

Wuppuluri, Shyam, and A. C. Grayling, eds. *Metaphors and Analogies in Sciences and Humanities: Words and Worlds*. Synthese Library 453. Cham: Springer, 2022.

www.ingramcontent.com/pod-product-compliance
Lightning Source LLC
Chambersburg PA
CBHW030857170426
43193CB00009BA/641